Mother, UNMERITED FAVOR

MARTHA GEARY

ISBN 978-1-64670-132-2 (Paperback)
ISBN 978-1-64670-133-9 (Digital)

Covenant Books, Inc.
11661 Hwy 707
Murrells Inlet, SC 29576
www.covenantbooks.com

I wanted to do this for the inspiration of my life, my God, my Jesus, and my sweet Holy Spirit who has been my rock and my foundation to where I stand. He has been a shelter from life's raging storms and my help in my times of need. There's never been a time in my life that he wasn't there. He's a friend so tried and true. After all, he loved me so much he died for me; even the hairs of my head are numbered. And he loves all of his children just as much. All I can say is, if you don't know him, seek him with all your heart. You'll never be sorry you did. I cannot comprehend a life without him.

He is my life; and without him, there is no life. I've poured out my heart in this material I've written. And when you read it, you'll have no problem realizing where my heart is and whom it belongs to.

I gave my heart and my life to my Lord and Savior at the age of twelve. I was a very shy young lady, but in a packed out church house, I got up out of my seat and started down the aisle to an old-fashioned altar to give my life to my Lord. About halfway there, I had an experience I'll never forget. *I met Jesus.* When the Bible says he is the light, trust me, *he is.* The light shined so brightly there in his presence that it blocked out everyone in that church, except Jesus and me. I know I was on my tiptoes trying with everything in me just to touch his hands.

There he stood in a white robe down to his feet; and he had his hands stretched out, palms up, beckoning me to come to him. I don't remember his face; all I remember are his hands and the overwhelming urgency to touch them. I'll never forget that experience—that encounter with my Lord as long as I live on the face of this earth.

It has touched my heart and my soul in a way I could never explain. It remains vivid in my mind as if it happened today or yesterday. Skeptics may say I was dreaming or hallucinating, but (1) I wasn't asleep; and (2) I was only a twelve-year-old child. I didn't know about all that other stuff. I just know what I saw and experienced that day in that church house. He's real to me, and he'll always be. These things I've written in this book are things he gives me that I want to share—his love toward me and my love for his creation. In other words, his sheep as we are called. He asked Peter, his disciple, "Do you love me, Peter?"

Peter replied, "Yes, Lord."

Jesus said, "Feed my sheep."

And that's the desire of my heart to feed the sheep of his pasture. So please, dear friend. As you read these words, have yourself a feast. God loves you. He loves everyone just as he loves me. It's not his will that anyone perish. As you read these words, I pray that you are touched by the Master's hands.

This book is also dedicated to my children that God blessed me with; and I feel I truly am blessed. My firstborn, Deborah Lynn; my second, Johnny Edward; my third, David Aaron; and my fourth, Deanna Dawn. My beautiful grandchildren: Brandon, Bradly, Shawn, Sarah, Nathaniel, Destini, Tyler, and Cody.

Step-grandchildren: Dustin and Jamie; Jamie is deceased. He passed from this life at only twenty-six years of age. This is dedicated to Kristy, Timothy, Kerrie, Scott, Tasha, and my one living sibling, Billy. Since this book, my sister Alpha passed away. Also, to the memory of the ones that have gone on ahead of me, my mother and daddy—Luther and Gertie Blanton. My brothers and sisters Wilodean, Edith, Leslie, Lealand, Lonard, Charles, Doris, Elaine, and Alpha.

As you can see, I came from a large family. I love each and every one of them and truly miss the ones that are gone. But time and our Savior have a way of healing all wounds. I only need to trust him.

Contents

Introduction

I, Martha Ann Blanton, was born on September 24 in Jefferson County, Kentucky (Louisville), to Luther Edward Blanton and Gertie Mae Blanton. I was born into a large family of eleven children, myself being the seventh child. Needless to say, there was never a dull moment around our home.

By the time I was around three years old, we lived in a place called *Gulf Hollow*. What a place that was—Edmonson County, Kentucky. At nighttime, it was dark as a dungeon down there. It was a big hole in the earth, and our little cabin sat by a creek that had what we called a walk log. This was the only way we had to cross the creek, and when that old creek would swell, we would have to leave our home and go visit relatives for a while.

The first tragedy that struck our family happened there. It was my first acquaintance with grief. My eldest brother Lealand, who was only seventeen years old at that time and was tired from the day's work, had gone swimming with a younger cousin in a place we called a quarry hole. It was a place where rock had been dug out, and it had filled with water. The hole was very deep and dangerous. But my brother, as I was told, was a very good swimmer.

Our young cousin who was not swimming ran as hard as he could to bring us the tragic news that Lealand had drowned. Even though I was very young, I shall never forget that day—watching my mother distraught and my dad walking the hollow grounds wailing like an animal. Those echoes were haunting. I don't know how we made it but by the grace of God. So at a very early age, I was acquainted with grief. We moved to many places after that, but the one I loved the most was Grayson County, Kentucky, in a small town known as Leitchfield.

Our home there was a two-story white house with a white picket fence around it. And, oh, there were roses at the gate—red ones—and a porch that stretched the length of the front of the house.

In back of the house, there stood a huge pear tree. The branches hung over the roof. Us children would go upstairs, climb out the window, pick the pears, and enjoy a meal of the most pleasant-tasting fruit. Of course, Mother didn't mind us picking and eating the pears; they were good for us. But she cautioned us to be very careful to not fall off the roof of the house.

Our mother was a protective mother, but she was not over-protective. She did not restrain us to the point that we could not enjoy life on the farm. Dad was the same way. He wanted us to enjoy our lives. But there were boundaries and rules, and we knew them well. And there were consequences of disobedience; we also knew that well.

Our dad was a very strict disciplinarian; the authority of our home, without a doubt, belonged to him. When he was away from home, our mother fell into that role and executed it with majesty, as did both of them. They both were godly parents, and I know the Bible was their guide to raising us children and the way they tried to live their lives. There was a lot of land with our farm. We had a large barn, smoke house, pigs, cows, chickens, horses, and mules Daddy plowed with.

It was a working farm, and my dad sure did work it from sunup to sundown along with my eldest brother Leslie. My family so reminded me of the *Waltons* as seen on TV in the 1970s to the '80s. We all loved the farm, and I'd venture to say that some of the happiest times of our lives were lived there. I used to walk behind Dad when he would be plowing with his team of mules. I loved to feel the just plowed earth beneath my bare feet; I loved that feeling. It was so fresh and new. The mules were very obedient. Just like us kids, they seem to know exactly what was expected of them and did it. My dad, bless his heart, could be as stubborn as those mules; and somehow, they just knew. Rebellion wasn't an option, as us children also knew.

He was a very stern man; but, oh, what a man he was. He would have willingly died for his wife and his children; I felt so safe in his presence. My mother was a meek, loving person who also gave her all for her husband and her children.

She always planted a large garden. I can picture her now hoeing in that garden. She always wore a bonnet on her head, shielding her from the hot sun as she worked. What a picture that was to me. It is forever etched in my childhood memory as was my dad plowing. There were so many events and so many memories there on that farm. I could write a beautiful book about it, and maybe someday, I will.

We moved away from the farm to our dismay; none of us wanted to leave, but we had to go. We moved to many places after that. Some were happy times, and some, not so happy. But our love for each other never faltered. We were a close bunch of siblings, and that spilled over in our adult life. My dad and mother are gone now and so are my four brothers and four sisters All that remain of our large family are my eldest sister Alpha, my youngest brother Billy, and myself. This book I'm writing now has been a long-time coming, something I've been wanting to do for so long.

My Testimony

My Lord, My God, My redeemer,
My God who has been with me
Since the day I was born into this world,
Who has been My strength, My life.
My Lord who has brought me through
All My trials, My tribulations, and sicknesses,
Who has shown his love and kindness to his servant.
He who has kept me from the evil,
Washed away all My sins.
How blessed and honored I am to be called his.
People look at me in amazement, they say,
"Ah, ah, surely God is with her.
"He keeps her with his Mighty arm,
"And none shall take her out of his hand.
"Blessed forevermore are his redeemed," and let them say so,
The testimony of my mouth will speak of
His marvelous grace all the days of my life.
His anchor still holds; what a mighty God I serve,
My Jesus, My friend, whose blood has been applied
To this his temple. Oh, my Lord, my rock
On which I stand, in whom I put my trust
Now and forevermore.
Surely, I will sing his praises
All the days of My life.
We overcome
By the blood of the Lamb
And by the word
Of our testimony.
(Revelation 12:10–11,17)

The Visit

When Jesus visited this old house
He knocked on the door of my heart
At first, I was afraid to let him in
There was so much darkness and sin within
What would he do if I answered the knock?
Would he walk back out and turn the lock?
Would he see the mess the house is in?
This house so dark and full of sin
Would he just say, "Oh what a mess
"What have you done, child?"
Can this house be blessed?
Well, with all uncertainty, I approached the door
Shivering and shaking like so many times before
Knock, knock, he's out there. "Oh, what must I do?"
He won't go away; he's steadfast and true
I'll answer this time; I won't turn him away
I'll not bid him come back
Or wait another day
I open the door; his brightness shines through
How wonderful this Savior
So steadfast and true
Immediately there in his presence
I fall to my knees; his voice cries out
"There's surely a need
"I can take this old house
"And make it brand-new
"The decision, my child
"It's all up to you."

The Master's Face

Lord, I don't know any fancy words to say
All I know is I'm here today
Because of your mercy and your grace
I only like from day to day
Just as a child, I rely on you
Somehow, I know your word is true
Each step I take, I'm trusting you
With a child-like faith to see me through
Just as the sparrow you watch each day
You watch my life in every way
The paths I take; Lord, sometimes, I stray
But your arm keeps me safe
And will guide me all the way
Sometimes, I stumble; and oft times, I fall
But, Lord, you were right there beside me
To guide me through it all
Your patience and kindness, your outstretched hands
Surpasses all this life could demand
Of one small child trying to run life's race
Trying desperately through it all
Just to see
The Master's race

Letter to My Father

My Father,

I want to talk with you. I want to tell you my innermost thoughts even though I know that you know everything about me. I still feel the need to express myself.

First of all, I want to thank you for loving me enough to send your Son to die for my sins. Even though it hurts you so to watch him hang there on that cross and suffer such shame and disgrace, oh, how you must have loved me.

When I think of how he suffered for my sins, he wore the crown of thorns that I should have worn. He felt the lashes of the whip that I should have felt. The blood gushed out of his side that should have fallen from mine and the nails that were driven through his hands and feet. It hurts me to think that this was happening because of my sins; he died for my sins. But, Father, the thing that I remember most is what he said while hanging there on that cross, "Father, forgive them for they know not what they do." How wonderful and kind my dear Savior is while he was yet dying, he thought only of me. How unselfish, how faithful and true.

Father, I love my Savior, just wanted you to know. So forgive me when I complain about some trivial thing that's happened during a day in my life. Give me the courage to bare my cross when troubles befall me. Let me not forget the price that was paid for me at Calvary. Help me to bare my crown of thorns with patience. Let me take my stripes without fear of the pain, and help me to remember that without them, there is no heavenly gain.

Let me not forget that we must be partakers in the death if we are to be partakers in the resurrection. So, Father, I give myself to you willingly as Christ gave himself willingly for me. Purge me, try me, and make me whole. And when it's all through, I pray that I may have a home up there with you.

Sometimes, I let the cares of this world tear me apart, but I'm glad that you know always what's first in my heart. When I'm sinking low, you're always there to lift me up. When you said you'd never leave me nor forsake me, I know it's the truth. Your promises are my foundation that I stand on. I take you at your word. There're so many times I have asked something of you and not much more than the words out of my mouth, and my prayers were answered.

Thank you for your kindness and your mercy and your steadfastness toward me. Help me to be as steadfast with you. Father, there're so much more I need to say to you, but I can't find the words to express what I feel in my heart, but I'm glad you know.

So I'll close now with all the love that's in my heart and my being. I want to be a daughter that you can be proud of. Forgive my shortcomings as I know you will, for you love me. Through my own children, I learned just how much I know you'll be right here with me through any and all trials I've yet to face and when it's all said and done. My Abba Father will be there to welcome me straight through those pearly gates of heaven 'cause my Father loves me.

Your daughter,
Martha

Faithful Soldier

I am a soldier in God's army
This old world is my battlefield
The enemy is known as old Satan
He comes to destroy kill and steal
His mission, he will accomplish if you give in to his will
There's plenty of souls that lay slaughtered
On this old battlefield
On this ground, there's blood-bought soldiers
Marching on through the toil and pain
Not much rest for these weary pilgrims
Marching on for their Lord and King
Weary soldier keep on marching
One soul is worth everything; fight the good fight for
    the Lord and the right
March on for your Lord and King
This battle we fight is not carnal
It's not fought with gun and knife
It's fought with love and compassion the love of Jesus
    Christ
He went to the cross to gain your pardon
He died there that you may be free
On that old rugged cross, he was crucified
He died there for you and me
So when I am in the heat of the battle
I remember the deed of God's only Son
How he came here to this old earth
And fought his battle till it was won
For me, the battle still rages; seems it goes on and on
    though I'm a wounded soldier
I'll keep on marching on

God called my name; he sent me out
I heard the battle call
The Lord's my strength; he'll be right there to see me
    through it all
Standing steadfast on the rock of ages
I know I'll never fall
Weary soldier, don't give up now
Rescue the soul that's in need
There's a gold crown laid up in heaven for the soldier
    that succeeds
This battle will soon be over now
Life's race on this earth is run
Look toward the heavens; faithful soldier, soon, you'll
    behold the face of God
And Jesus his only Son who's seated at the right hand
    of his Father
Upon his heavenly throne

I'll Stand by You

When you're lost and lonely and no one seems to care
I'll stand by you
When heartache and grief you need to share
I'll stand by you
When the world's an awful place
Just look up behold my face
It's there you'll find pure love and grace
I'll stand by you
When all others let you down
I'll stand by you
When not a true friend can be found
I'll stand by you
I'll stick closer than a brother
I carried your cross upon my shoulders
No truer love can ever be found
I'll stand by you
I'll stand by you when all else is gone

I'll stand by you when you're all alone
Child, all you need do is call my name
I'll stand by you
I'll stand by you through the fiery furnace
I'll be right here in the lion's den
Just call my name when you need a friend
I'll stand by you
When you cross old Jorden's chilly tide
I'll be right there right by your side
Till you reach the other side
I'll stand by you
I'll stand by your till you're safely home
No, I'll never leave you here all alone
Until your last breath on this earth is gone
Until you're singing around God's throne
I'll stand by you

The Road

Bitterness has taken hold of my life—anger, misery, heartache, and strife. Sometimes, don't even know who I am while desperately seeking the Great I Am. I know that Jesus could heal me today. But somehow, can't seem to find the way. The road is rocky and full of holes. I'm traveling too fast I'm losing control, travelling too fast down this rocky road. Can anyone stop this weary soul? Slow down. I hear a small voice say, "You're going too fast. That isn't the way."

"Can't find the brakes," I seem to reply. I guess I've lost the reason why my heart is sinking as soon as I go traveling too fast down this rocky road. Anger and misery are life's potholes. As wearily, wearily onward I go, I can't even turn to the left or to the right. Where are the signs?

No day here; no night. "Lord," my soul cries out, "where have you gone? Can't seem to find you. I'm too far from home." This is a lonely old road; did I choose well, or did I make a wrong turn? This road seems like hell. Poverty, sickness, toil, and strife here on this road is the way of life. I can travel this road if I know you're there. Your light will guide me through all the snares.

So take my hand and lead me home straight to my Father's open arms where the weary pilgrims all find rest in that haven of hope on my Father's breast. Resting peacefully on my Father's breast. "My child, I'll never leave you nor forsake you till you find your way home. No, I'll never leave you on this road alone."

I Thirst

Jesus, thou Son of David
I call out your name
Among the pain and heartache, you are with me once again
I hear your voice you stand still
And command me to be called
I cast aside my garment
I come running to you
And on my knees, I fall
Through tear-filled eyes, I look up to you
And then you softly say
"What would thou that I should do unto thee"
With broken heart in desperation
I reply
"Oh, Jesus. I need a drink of water. I thirst
"I'm hungry. I need to be fed
"My body needs your healing touch
"In you, I need to rest
"Oh, Jesus, I need a friend
"I feel so all alone
"I need for you to be with me
"Until you take me home
"I need your strength to lift me up
"Lest I faint along this way
"I need you to open my blinded eyes
"So I can see you day by day
"Open the doors of heaven
"And rain down your blessings upon me, Lord
"So I may walk your way

"I want to see the streets of gold
"And walk with you some day
"Oh, Jesus, I ask of you these things
"Send them all my way
"If I remain a little while
"I thank you, Lord, my own
"You are the giver of my life
"Oh, Lord, I trust in you alone"

My Mission and Goal

In this life down here on earth

We're running to and fro

Trying so hard to please our Lord

Not knowing which way to go

What am I here to do, oh, Lord?

What is my mission and goal?

Am I sinking fast in the miry clay?

Staining the depths of my weary soul?

Teach me the way that I must go

Don't let me stray down here below

Stand beside me through each trial

It's only you I trust and know

Stop Striving, My Child

Oh, Lord, what am I to do?

I try so very hard to please you

To live a just and upright life

Seems the harder I try

The farther away I get from the perfect me

I'm trying so hard to be

Seems you just say

"Stop striving, My child

"I know who you are

"I knew you before I called you

"To be part of my kingdom

"Do you think anything you do

"Or say surprises me?"

I know you love me, Lord

But for the life of me

I don't see how you can

The things I don't want to do

Are the very things I do?

And the things I want to do, I don't

This is a letter that I wrote to President Obama. I felt in my heart I should write to him since I have heard that Obama is Moslem or Muslim. I don't know how this letter will be received. As I felt led to write it, the words I put on paper speak of love, not hatred. Pray fully it will be accepted as such, a letter of love to our fellowman. To our president who is governing our United States.

If he reads this letter, I do hope he comes to know our God of this universe who is love and who teaches us to love, not hate.

Mr. President & First Lady,

Allow me to introduce myself. My name is Martha Geary, born of Luther & Gertie Blanton of Edmonson County, Kentucky. I am the seventh of eleven children. Not of any high status in this world, but I am a child of the Most High God. I was born again through Jesus Christ, his Son, and had been through some very trying times in my life as I'm sure most of the population of this old world has been.

I really don't feel I'm special, only to my Lord, but I've been a dreamer all my life. Dreams and visions have been a part of my life since I can remember. My head hits the pillow, I fall asleep. I'm immediately taken to another world. It is so real; I'm there. I don't pretend to be smart, but I'm certainly not ignorant. I'm not a psychic. I don't believe in that. I'm just a normal everyday human being who was taught about my Lord all my life.

I say I was born of fire and water, my dad being fire and my mother being water. When my dad walked into a room, authority was there. We did not question that; none of us. God's way of living was his way. I was raised by a Bible in one of his hands and a razor strap in his other. I and the rest of his children respected him. I love and miss him dearly. He is deceased, and so is my mother. I love and miss them both.

My mother, on the other hand, was a very meek person but stood her ground when she believed in something. She was a very loving person. Life without her guidance has been pretty rough at times. She was our strong tower in troubled times. I believe, still today, her prayer is with me, my sister, and brother who are also alive.

My dad was a hard worker. In my earlier days, he was a farmer, working from sunup to sundown. As a child, I remember walking behind him when he was plowing with his team of mules, feeling the just plowed earth on my bare feet. In my eyes, he was Samson. His strength was unmatchable straight from God. He never backed down from any man and would have died for his family.

My mother was a housewife all her married life; my dad wouldn't have had it any other way. She was definitely lady of the house and was to be honored as such; there was no question about that either. Were they perfect human beings? No, but in my eyes, they were very close. My dad could be a hard man sometimes, but he had a hard life. It made him tough. He was a man, when men were men.

I grew up knowing what authority was and respecting it. My parents taught me that way, and my Bible tells me to. There is no one in authority that God didn't ordain to be there for his purpose and not their own.

I believe that man in his lack of wisdom doesn't understand this. There's nothing that happens on the face of this earth that God doesn't know about. He created earth, and he created man and every living thing whether they realize it or not. Everything that happens, he ordains it to be so. God is above every power that is in heaven or in earth. The problem I see is this, there's no fear of God in man's eyes. If there was, they would be doing things his way and not their own. They don't reverence him as God, and they are trying their best to take him out of everything. But it will not happen. He is the head and will always be. And his Word is truth. What he said in his Word will be, and opposing that will only lead to disaster for them. And when they are in a position of authority, needless to say, their decisions can only have devastating consequences for people they are governing.

But God will allow this to continue only for a season. Look what happened to King Nebuchadnezzar in the Old Testament. He exalted himself, gave himself glory, and did not reverence God. He wound up growing long fingernails and eating grass like an animal.

God knows how to abase those who try to lift themselves above him. I challenge you to read the Bible for yourself. Personally, I cut my teeth on the King James Version and will not read those other revised additions. Every time man revises something, they wound up watering down the Word or truly losing something in the translation. My take on revised editions. Revelations warns us of adding to or taking from his Word.

I know this is a long letter, but the Lord lay upon my heart words to say, and I must say them. What good are we to him or anyone else if we can't obey? My prayer for you both is that you listen to God and obey his commands. Do not listen to evildoers who devise evil upon their beds and intends to destroy our nation and will use you as a tool. It wasn't man that put you in authority even though it may seem so. It was the God of this universe, and you are there for his divine purpose not to kill, steal, and destroy. The Word of God plainly says that is Satan's mission. The earth is Satan's playground. People, for their lust for power and greed, fall under the influence of Satan's evil when he accomplishes his will in them. And through them, his reward for them, is a burning hell. That's all he has to offer. God says he came that you may have life and have it more abundantly.

Mr. President, whom are you serving? Hopefully and prayerfully, our Lord. Seek his face. Only through his Son, Jesus Christ, can you get to heaven. He is the Way, the Truth, and the Life.

Long life and peace is what he offers you here on this earth, and a beautiful heaven is your reward when you leave here. God is love, not hatred; and all who love are of God.

Tell me if you can. Who, in their right mind, would want to serve a being they call God who only teaches hatred and destruction and death to their fellow man? The true God of our universe teaches love. He is love. And anyone who knows him knows love.

PS: I challenge you to meditate on what I've written here for you.

Sincerely,
Martha Geary

The Candy Store

Today I came to my Father in heaven
Like a child would go to their daddy to ask questions about things they
    don't understand
I said, "Father, in this world"
"I feel like a child in a candy store"
"I see all the delicious things I'd love so much to have"
"My mouth watering for the treats"
But my Father says, "No, you cannot touch them"
"Sweetheart, they're filled with poison"
"You see, old Satan put them there to entice you"
"It's like a stranger that I have warned you"
"Not to take candy from"
This is the way the Lord so lovingly answered my questions and from his
    wisdom
I saw clearly the world and all the things
Satan has placed in it to lure us away from our Father in heaven and
    that city paved with gold
You see, all old Satan has to offer is hell
He makes this old world look so good
This is his candy store
God placed Adam and Eve in the beautiful Garden of Eden and told
    them
"Do not eat of the tree of life, or you will die"
Satan lies and tells Eve, "It won't hurt you"
Oh, my child; if God says, "Don't partake of it"
Don't; it's full of Satan's poison; God doesn't lie
Satan is your enemy; he would love nothing
More than for you to believe his lies that will send your soul on a down-
    ward spiral that will snare you and destroy you
He comes only for these reasons
To kill, steal, and destroy
See the world clearly for what it is
Satan's Candy store of poison
Don't partake of it

I Don't Have Time for You, Satan

I don't have time to whine and cry
I don't have time for the pain
I don't have time for old Satan and all the things
*   he tries to bring*
I know he comes to kill steal and destroy
From him, I don't need a thing
So why is he here? I ask myself
He's certainly not a welcome guest
He's here to take my life if he can; that's that old
*   demon's quest*
Does he think he can gain control of me by put-
*   ting me to the test?*
Doesn't he know that Jesus has already been here?
And on that solid rock is where I rest
So Satan, I don't have time for your misery
I don't have time for your pain
I don't have time for all the things
Your wretched demon self brings
So you just be on your way of you; I'm not afraid
Jesus died to give me life

I know I'll walk his way

*The path I chose is straight and narrow that will
  lead me to him someday*

*He built the strength within me and said, "Now
  overcome." And he said to me, "Now don't be
  afraid"*

The battle has been won

He gave me power to tread on serpents

And power over death, hell, and the grave

If all these things he built within me

If I am who I say I am in him

No, I'll never be afraid

I don't have time to whine and cry

I don't have time for your pain

I don't have time for your wretched demon self

Satan and all the misery that you bring

So you just get on out of here, just be on your way

Jesus came that I may have life

And, yes, he's here to stay

You Were Always There

When I was just a little child
You were always there
Jesus, you were my best friend
Through the heartache, sorrow, and fear
I don't know why I was so alone with my brothers and sis-
    ters around
But when it came down to a best friend
You were the best one I ever found
I would look for you up high in a tree I'd climb
Or just lying on the ground
Just staring up in the heavens
You were always around
Momma told me about you through the Bible
She would read
She said if I would accept you into my heart, you would fill
    my every need
When I became a little older
I took my mother's advice
And in a church house filled with people
Jesus, I ask you into my life
Clearly, I remember the beating of my heart

How wildly and passionately it beat for you

Right from the very start

I knew from that day forward

You'd never leave me alone

The instant you came into my life, this child had found her home

My life has been through many trials

Heartaches and despair, mountain tops, and valleys

But you were always there sinking low on shifting sand

You'd pull me out and take my hand

I love my rock on which I stand you were always there

You were always there to love and comfort me and if I make
    my bed in hell

Right there is where you'll be

If I take my flight to heaven

Anywhere my life may lead

I know you'll be right there beside me

To fulfill my every need

Jesus, I love my rock on which I stand

And you were always there

Send Your Light to Me

Chorus:
When I'm lost on life's stormy sea
Lord, send your light to me
When it seems I've lost my way
Lord, send your light to me
When your still small voice I cannot hear
By your spirit draw me near
When I need you ever near
Lord, send your light to me
1ˢᵗ Verse:
When old Satan sets his snares
Lord, send your light to me
When I'm lost and no one cares
Lord, send your light to me
When my cross grows heavy
And my burdens I must bare
I know how much you care
Lord, send your light to me
(Repeat Chorus)
2ⁿᵈ Verse:
I set my eyes toward glory land
Lord, send your light to me
I won't rest until I'm there
Lord, send your light to me
This narrow path I'm treading on
Lord, send your light to guide me home
Light my way that I may see
Lord, send your light to me
(Repeat Chorus)

Awesome God

I hear the thunder
As it clashes around me
I see the lightening
As it lights up the dark sky
I see your fearful and awesome power, Lord—
As you shake the heavens
Our God of the heavens cannot be denied
Your power is fearful to those who don't know you
But I see the love that you have for me
Your perfect love cast all fear aside
As with your mighty hand you lovingly guide
As you calm the universe
And you calm the fear I'm feeling inside
Awesome God of the universe
He watches over me
During the dark storms, I know right where he'll be
Seated on his throne way up there on high
Comforting me with his still small voice sending me rainbows by
and by
Awesome God of the universe
He don't want to see me cry
I hear the thunder
As it clashes around me
I see the lightening as it lights up the dark sky
I see your fearful and awesome power, Lord—
As you shake the heavens
Our God of the heavens cannot be denied

I'll Worship You

Though the storm clouds rage
You'll be by my side
Nothing on earth to fear
I know you'll be my guide
In this barren land
Or on life's foreign sod wherever my feet may trod
Oh, Son of the living God
I'll worship you; I'll worship you
No matter what others do
Oh, Son of God, I will worship you
Let me sing a new song of this mercy and his grace
Let me tell of things he's done
Someday I'll see his face
I'll look upon the one who saved me by his grace
The one I long to see
Yes, I'll bow down on my knees
No matter what others do
Oh, Son of God, I'll worship you; I'll worship you
Yes, King of glory; I'll worship you
Worthy are you to be praised who took my sins away
When my feet were on life's sinking sand
Your voice cried out, "Come, take my hand"
There, the blood poured over me
The lamb was slain to set me free
In this barren land
Oh, Son of God, you took my hand
I'll worship you; I'll worship you
Oh, Lamb of God, I'll worship you
Backup singers singing "I Will Worship You"

Jump and I Will Catch You

The mighty eagle will take her little one to the highest peak
She will soar way up high
And drop her little one from her beak
Her sharp eyes are ever watching
To see if it will fly
Then she'll swoop down with her mighty claws
And catch it, so it won't die
Sometimes, I feel like the eaglet
Who's trying so hard to fly
Fearing so much to try my wings
Afraid that I might die
The world has been a hurtful place
You've taken me to great heights
You've set me on the mountain top
And bid me there to fly
Jump and I will catch you
I promise, my child, you won't die
Jump and I will catch you
If you will only trust me
I'll teach you how to fly

Pass It On; Pass It On Down

When you've found a ray of sunshine
Pass it on
When you were lost but now you're found
Pass it on; pass it on down
Love is nothing till you give it away
'Til you can bring hope to another one's day
When happiness is here to stay
Pass it on
When you have found that pot of gold
Pass it on; pass it on down
When you see a needy soul
And you have riches here untold
Don't just keep it all to yourself
Pass it on to someone else
Pass it on; pass it on down
There's hurting people everywhere
Just waiting for someone out there to care
I beg you
Don't keep love all to yourself
Just pass it on to someone else
Pass it on; just pass it on down
Love is nothing 'til you give it away
'Til you can bring hope to another one's day
When happiness is here to stay
Pass it on; pass it on down

Over Jordan's Banks

Over Jordan's Banks, he waits for me
His voice I clearly hear tenderly calling out to me
Drawing me ever near
I'll step into that pure, clean water
And to the other side I'll go
Over Jordan's Banks he waits for me where the milk and honey
flows
The light ahead is getting brighter now
A smile on his face I see
With arms outstretched he bids me come
My Savior welcomes me
I see his face; I touch his hands
And on my knees, I bow down low
I kiss his feet in reverence there
As my Savior washed me white as snow
My friend, let me tell you something
I believe you need to hear
It's all about this man across Jordan
Who's waiting for you there
His voice is tenderly calling you
Oh, listen can't you hear
With outstretched arms, he bids you come
The Savior wants you near
Over Jordan's Banks, he waits for you
His voice I pray you hear
Tenderly calling out to you
Drawing you ever near
Please step into that pure clean water
And to the other side you'll go
Over Jordan's Banks, he waits for you
Where the milk and honey flows
My friend, I hope to see you there where the milk and honey
flows

Twelve Legions of Angels

Do you not know I could have called twelve Legion
of Angels?
Do you not know I could have come down from that
tree?
With broken heart, my Father looked down from
heaven
He turned his head as your sin covered me
There, the cross lay heavy upon my shoulders
There, they placed a crown of thorns upon my head
No comfort, no kind words that day was spoken
As the soldiers marched me up to Calvary's hill
Do you not know why I suffered and I died there?
Do you not know why I hung there on that tree?
Did you not hear my voice as I called you?
As my weakened voice called out to you from Calvary
Do you not know I could have called twelve Legion
of Angels?
Do you not know I could have come down from that
tree?
With broken heart, my Father looked down from heaven
He turned his head as your sin covered me
There, my blood was spilled that day at Calvary
Your sins were covered by the pain that I bore
I was the Lamb sacrificed for your pardon
I did it all so you could live forevermore
I did it all so you could live forevermore

Life

I've lived a life of sorrow. My body has known some pain,
my mind has been so scattered
I cry, oh, Lord, who is to blame?
From birth, my trials begun, Lord
The first breath I took you gave
I came into this old world so helpless
No way to take control
Left to the cared of my parents, to be cared for, so I could
grow
My dad was oft times angry. For what reason? I did not know
I wanted so much to be loved by him, but his love he could
not show
My mother, a humble and quiet one
A meek spirit she did possess
I wondered what would become of me
Oh, Lord, I was put to the test
As I grew and grew and learned of you
I knew somehow that I'd been blessed
Through these special parents you left me with
Oh, yes, surely, I'm truly blessed
I won't think of the times I didn't understand the wisdom
of your plan
I'll just think of the times you stood me up and gave me
strength to stand
The times you dried each tear that feel
Each time you made me see, demons flee at your command
Each time I feel down on my knees and touched your
outstretched hand

Crossing Over

Chorus
Someday soon, I'll be crossing over
to that land on the other shore
I won't have no troubles and trials
All of life's sorrows will soon be ore

Verse 1
Don't build for me no fine mansions
down here on earth with its toils and strife
Soon, I'll be in the clouds of glory
where I'll have a brand-new life

Chorus
Someday soon, I'll be crossing over
to that land on the other shore
I won't have no troubles and trials
All of life's sorrows will soon be ore

Verse 2
So carry on when I have parted
Don't weep for me; I'm going home
No sad farewells; just know I'm happy
In my home on the other shore
(Repeat chorus and last line of chorus)

Won't You Be Ready?

Chorus
Won't you be ready when Jesus comes?
Just give your heart to God's only Son
He'll love you and lead you every step of the way
So won't you give your heart to Jesus today?

Verse 1
The sinner is standing in God's judgment today
But he made a way for all to be saved
He loved you so much he sent Jesus to die
He'll save you today; God's Word does not lie

Chorus
So won't you be ready when Jesus comes?
Just give your heart to God's only Son
He'll love you and lead you every step of the way
Won't you give your heart to Jesus today?

Verse 3
I'm standing here pleading his mercy is great
If you don't repent, you can't walk through those gates
Hell is for sinners; this will be your fate
Please give your heart to Jesus today
(Repeat chorus)

The Soldier

I am a soldier so far from home
Lonely and forgotten, battle-scarred and worn
Fighting a battle I did not choose
Fighting for our freedom we can't afford to lose
Comrades falling to my left and to my right
Can't stop to see if they're dead or alive
So I keep pressing forward; I hear the battle cry
Onward to victory whether I live there or die
Wounded and weak now will I ever see home
Soldiers pass on by me leaving me there alone
I awake to a brightness am I dead or alive
I see people standing around me trying hard to
    revive
What life I have left so broken inside
They sent me home to a land I know well
The land that I fought for through living hell
What will I do now? So wounded and weak
With a wife and three children
I can't think now; I can't speak.
Years pass by; now I've recovered
At least that's what they say, but the battle it
    still goes on
I fight it every day. Doctors and clinics, pills for
    the pain
Bills piling up; heartsick once again
Don't look at me and pity what you see

Just common courtesy is all that I need
A home in the country to call my very own
With God's help, I'll make it, after all
He's the one who brought me safely back home
No, it's not pride; I'm just here to say
It's just a wounded soldier still fighting his battles
Minute by minute still, day by day
So if you see a soldier pass by you on the street
Walking with two legs or in a wheelchair with
    no feet
Take a minute and salute him, truly if you please
Let him know you care about the wound there
    on his feet
Let him know you care about
The price he paid to keep us free
Let him know that he's still loved
Here in this country
Home of the brave, still, land of the free
Thanks to our soldiers
Who paid the price, who gave his all
For you and for me
No greater love has no man
Than one who will lay down
His life for a friend

When Jesus is All I've Got, He's All I Need

When he's all I've got, he's all I need
When he's all I've got, he's all I need
When my backs against the wall
There's no way out, no way at all
When Jesus is all I've got, he's all I need
When he's all I've got, he's all I need
When Jesus is all I've got, he's all I need
When no one else can be found
When life has pushed me to the ground
When he's all I've got, he's all I need
When the doctors say there is no way
I may not live to see another day
Jesus comes and lifts me up
And lets me sip there from his cup
Smiles and says, "Child it's okay"
Through faith, you'll live to a ripe old age
When he's all I've, got he's all I need
Jesus whispers in my ears
Those beautiful words I long to hear
Faith can move a mountain you see
Let go of it all; just trust in me
I'll be your beacon in the night
When your heart it knows such fright
I am your guiding light; I'm all you need
When Jesus is all I've got, he's all I need

Supping with My Father

Sometimes, numbness takes me over

life as I know it seems, oh, so unreal

I cry out in agony

Lord, hear my humble plea

Take me to that place with you

Where it's only you and me

There, we sup together

My fainted heart knows rest

It's in that place where your children go

Where Father always knows what's best

With outstretched arms, you bid me come

And rest my weary head

And then when I have to leave you again

It's the leaving that I dread

But I'll be back to you real soon

To rest my weary head

Way Up High

Chorus:
Way up high I'll see my Savior face-to-face
Way up high in that land of endless day
where God's angels behold his face
In that land of endless day way up high
We'll toss our crowns at God's feet
As we walk on golden streets
where the curbs there do play
In that land of endless day
way up high
There, we'll gather around God's throne
In that city where we call home
Never no more to roam
way up high
There, no thief will enter
I'll be washed clean of my sins
way up high
When I climb those golden stairs
I'm going to that city built four square
where I'll see all my loved ones there
No more heartache, no more care
way up high

Kiss the Hurt and Make It Go Away

To brother Billy

When I was just a little boy
It seemed so long ago
I'd run and play till it got dark
Until I couldn't see
I'd dash my foot against a stone
Mom would run and pick me up
And set me on her knee
She'd look real hard at the little scrape
And softly say to me
"I'll kiss the hurt and make it go away
"Jesus and I will make it better
"Just you wait and see"
I always believed what Momma said
I know she'd never lie
She'd gently wipe away my tears
And hold me when I cried
Those days are gone; I feel so alone
Still dashing my feet against the stones
But Momma's not here to pick me up
And kiss the hurts away
But Jesus still walks beside me
And I know he'll be there always
To pick me up when I fall down
To put my feet on solid ground
To kiss the hurts; to heal my pains
He'll stay beside till the end

Into His Hands

Chorus
Into his hands, I commit my spirit
There's no other place I'd rather be
Into his hands, he'll ever keep me
Safe in his bosom, I'll always be

Verse 1
No matter where this life may lead me
No matter how many roads I may trod
My savior is always there to protect me
I'll never stray too far from my God

Verse 2
Through his spirit, his love guides me
His wisdom too far above my reach
I call to him for understanding
To his children, his love he'll teach

Chorus
Into his hands, I commit my spirit
There's nowhere else I'd rather be
Into his hands, he'll ever keep me
Safe in his bosom I'll always be

Verse 3
Through his son, he draws me to him
The way of life the Lord has shown
No one else above or below him
No one else for my sins will atone
Through my trials, he's right beside me

I know I'll never be alone
I know his love will always guide me
Until he brings me safely home

Into his hands, I commit my spirit
Until he brings me safely home

Who Loves You?

People, do you hear me?
Who loves you? Who loves me?
Who died for you on an old rugged cross?
That day at Calvary, who died for the lost?
Who was beaten for our transgressions?
Who was bruised for our iniquity?
Who made the lame to walk?
And who caused the blind to see?
Who rebuked the wind?
And who calmed the stormy sea?
Who did this all for you and for me?
Who fed five thousand
with three loaves of bread and two fishes?
Who walked on the water?
And who granted our wishes?
Who rose again straight from the dead?
On the third day just so he said
And as he said, he'll be back again
From the eastern sky, he will descend
The trumpet will sound before he appears
So people get ready, so there won't be no fears
He'll have on his vesture dipped in blood
Yes, he's coming back for the ones that he loves
King of all Kings, Lord of all Lords
The battle is his; he's going to make war
Who is this King that I'm speaking of?
This is our Jesus; yes, this is our Lord
People, who loves you?
Who do you love?
Jesus, Jesus
Jesus our Lord

Jesus, You're My Everything

For Johnny

I try so hard to say just what you mean to me
The words are hard to convey
for Jesus, you're my everything
As a child, I could not quite understand
circumstances and life's demands
I knew there was someone who guided my way
that walked beside me day by day
I felt your touch each time I cried
each time my heart would break inside
The road seemed rocky and, oh, so long
but you were always there right beside me
You lifted me up and made me strong
You instilled in me the strength to go on
When times were hard and things went wrong
Who could love me more than you?
Jesus my friend, tried and true
You're the breath that I breathe
The rock that I stand on
The refuge from life's perilous storm
You're my beacon in the night
You're my guide when I've lost my way
Jesus, you're my everything

Abundant Life

What is living, Lord?

It sure is not what I'm doing

You said you came

That I could have abundant life

The abundant life is not what I'm living

If it's something depending on me, Lord

I surely must be doing something wrong

So wrong

Nothing that feels this wrong

Can't be right

Oh, please, help me, Lord, to fight

I need the abundant life

Just to Be

I wonder what it's like just to be
Oh, I wonder what it's like to be free
From the struggles of this life
Free from toils free from strife
Oh, I wonder what it's like just to be
Oh, I wonder why I came into this world
To this prison camp of life was born a girl
To a low and lonely home always feeling so alone
Oh, I wonder why I came into this world
I wonder what it's like just to be
Oh, I wonder what it's like to be free
From the struggles of this life
Free from toils free from strife
Oh, I wonder what it's like just to be
Lord, you told me in your Word you'd set me free
Lord, you taught me in your Word just to be
Help me make your Word my own
Teach me, guide me to be strong
So I'll know just what it's like just to be
Help me lay my burdens at your feet
Teach me how to love and be free
Help me wear a smile
Through these long and bitter trials
Lord, teach me what it's like to be free
Oh, I know what it's like just to be
Oh, I know what it's like to be free
Jesus came into my life
Saved me from this life of sin
Now I know what it's like just to be
Praise God I know what it's like to be free

Behold, Child, How Much I Love You

A sight to behold your creation, Lord,
Your children have it all, so much beauty.
The roar of the ocean; the waves standing tall,
Coming to shore to crash upon it,
The sound it makes in the process; so serene.
How beautiful your creation, Lord, the sound!
Is music to my ears, soothing as though to say,
"My most precious creation, my child."
I put this here to say, "I love you" this beauty,
These sounds are for your pleasure.
The little birds outside my window, they sing to me,
Their sweet song, their lullaby soothes an aching heart,
Or brightens the darkest day.
The majestic mountains stand so tall,
Oh, my panting heart takes flight.
Rising higher and higher to the highest peak,
Like a mighty eagle spreading her wings.
And soaring above it all as though she hears the
Master's call, "Come with me; be free."
The sun beams bursting through the clouds,
As though heaven opened up, and your brightness
Shines through. It speaks to my heart.
"Oh, child, behold, how much I love you."
In the stillness of the night,
When everything is settled and quiet.
You come to me and sup with me,
Your gentle ways, your small still voice I hear,
A million words cannot express the love I feel
when I'm in your presence.
The awesome God of the universe

Takes time just for me; you numbered the hairs on my
head. My life it is so precious to you.
I love to dance and sing for you, Lord
I love to be your child who runs to your
waiting open arms and rest there in your bosom.
I know what you meant when you said in your Word,
"Unless you come as humble as a child
"You cannot see heaven." I love being your child,
And there in your presence is heaven.
As I dance and sing for you, I visualize
you sitting there on your throne
smiling down on me with the look of love
and adoration on your face
clapping your hands and tapping your feet
As I dance for my Father
I cannot contain my love when I hear that
Heavenly beat and enter your presence
David, you quoted as being a man after your
own heart, danced for you before the ark
of the covenant, Father; I know why.
David said of you, "My heart pants after you
"As the deer after the water brook"
And, yes, my Father. So does mine

The Oak and the Willow

The storm is raging
In the midst stands
A Willow tree
The Willow bows herself as in reverence
To the mighty force that has it caught
In its clutches, bending and swaying
She survives the storm
Because she knows how to bend
The mighty force does not break her
The same storm is raging
Caught in the clutches of the storm
There stands the majestic Oak tree
Standing very tall and straight
Refusing to bow, refusing to submit
To the force that has it in its clutches
It breaks and falls to the ground
Its strength becomes its weakness in the end
If only the Oak knew how to stand and bend
To let its strength work for it
And not against it
But the Oak does not know how to bend
The moral of this story is:
Sometimes, we need to know how to be an Oak
Sometimes, we need to know how to be a Willow
We can take lessons from them both
When we are in a heated discussion with someone
We need to learn when to bend and when to stand firm
When to let it go and when to show love and compassion by
submitting
Jesus knew this: "Love always ruled"
But sometimes he stood his ground and told them exactly
Who and what they were
Sometimes he is an Oak

Sometimes he is a Willow
Love, Mercy, Grace, Kindness, Forgiveness, Long suffering—
Is what Jesus is—Oak or Willow
Lord, let me learn how and when to be an Oak
Teach me when to stand straight and tall
For you, not to bend in the face of adversity
But, Father, also, let me learn to be a Willow
That I can bow and bend
In any situation I may be confronted with
Let Mercy, Grace, Kindness, Forgiveness and Long-suffering
Be everything that I am
Because that's what you are—whether Oak or Willow

A True Servant's Heart

Many false prophets have gone out before
Saying they are of you
I wonder if they truly know what they really do
Preaching and singing everywhere
For money and for fame
As for me, I don't care if anyone knows my name
It seems to be just for fame; I just don't understand
Why we should seek the glory of it all
When it's all about the man
The man who gave his life for us upon a cruel cross
The man who died that we may live
He gave his life there for the lost
So let me give my all for you because you gave your all for me
That people may know the reason why
You died to set the captive free
Search me and know me, oh, Lord
If I am truly what I should be
Then take this servant who longs to serve you
With a contrite spirit, I'll serve only thee
I don't want to go, Lord, for fortune or for fame
I just want to go, Lord, to lift up thy holy name
So if the world starts crowding in to snare my soul away
I'm confident you'll send your spirit
To light and guide my way
Examine me, oh, Lord, to see if I am true
Make my being an instrument to serve only you
Let me go in awe of my God so tried and true
I just want my heart to be
An instrument for you

The Lord Liveth and Blessed Be My Rock

The Lord liveth and blessed be my rock
And let the God of my salvation be exalted
His going forth is from the ends of the heaven,
And his circuit unto the end of it:
And there is nothing hid from the heart there of
The law of the Lord is perfect converting the soul:
The testimony of the Lord is sure, making wise the simple
The Lord liveth and blessed be my rock
And let the God of my salvation be exalted
The statutes of the Lord are right, rejoicing the heart
The commandment of the Lord is pure enlightening the eyes
The fear of the Lord is clean enduring forever
The judgments of the Lord are true and righteous altogether
More to be desired are they than gold,
Yeah, than much fine gold:
Sweeter also than honey and the honeycomb
The Lord liveth and blessed be my rock
And let the God of my salvation be exalted

Come On, Children
(Let's rock this world)

Come on, children, let's rock this world today
Let's tell everybody we know about Jesus
Let's sing about the one we love
Who sent his blessings from above
The one who died to set us free
He gave his life for you and me
With outstretched arms, he bids you come
So come on, children, let's rock this world today
Let's tell everybody we know about Jesus
He led us out of bondage
It's by his power we stand
I love to sing his praises; come on and take my hand
Let's walk this road together
We're headed for the Promised Land
Come on, children, let's rock this world today
Let's tell everybody we know about Jesus
If we band together in love
Stand tall and never run
Lift up our voices from coast to coast stand tall and
overcome
Jesus is our friend; he'll be with us till the end
On his promise we can depend
Let's tell everybody we know about Jesus

We won't back down in the face of trouble
Our hearts are set to follow you
We'll bare our cross straight up to Calvary
We're marching through we're the chosen few
We're going through no matter the cost
We're marching on to seek the lost
So come on, children let's rock this world today
Let's tell everybody we know about Jesus
Satan you're a defeated foe
You tell us lies try to steal our souls
You bring us down and cause us shame
No, we won't play your foolish games
Come on, children, let's rock this world today
Let's tell everybody we know about Jesus

The Master's Hands

Master, come touch this poor, wretched soul
Rest in your bosom there, make my abode
Master, I'm yielding to those unseen hands
More grace I'll receive at your blessed command
I was chipped and was marred without no one
to care
Lost and so lonely without hope of repair
I went down to the potter's house
Stood there at the wheel
Waiting to be molded to the potter's own will
Come shape me and mold me, oh, Master, today
As only you can in your loving sweet way
The clay is now ready to yield to those hands
And I'll be made whole at the potter's command
Oh, Master, come touch this poor, wretched soul
Rest in your bosom there make my abode
Master, I'm yielding to those unseen hands
More grace I'll receive at your blessed command
Yes, more grace I'll receive at your blessed
command

Momma, We Miss You

Momma, you're gone; and, oh, how we miss you

When you went away it hurts us so

You're the one who taught us about Jesus

It seems only yesterday

But it was many years ago

Not many earthly treasures down here did you possess

But the heavenly ones with wisdom were the ones you

always stressed to a brood of little children

Nestled closely to your breast

Given by the heavenly Father

Those were the ones that you loved best

He instilled in you the wisdom to teach us about him

This large brood of children

No, your eyes were never dimmed

He must have known the patients

So much you'd have to give

This kind of love and parents could only come from him

Jesus must have given you lots of faith

To teach to us his loving way

How many times we've seen you pray

For a fever to break, and it would go away

We trust him completely we wanted to say

Because of your teaching, Mother, you did it God's way

Or how many times you've prayed for food

When there wasn't enough to feed your hungry brood

Yes, you'd kneel right down on your knees

A knock came at the door, and there the food would be

Sometimes, these days when we think of you

It makes us very sad

But knowing you're home with the one that you love

For that part it makes us glad

And, Momma, please say hello to Dad

So, Jesus, take good care of our Momma

As we know most assuredly, you will

'Cause when she was here on this old earth

For you, her life she lived

Walk with her by the crystal river

And let her feet walk those streets of pure gold

Let Momma know the joy of being with her blessed Savior

The one that she loved so

Precious Blood of Jesus

Oh, precious blood of Jesus
Oh, come pour over me
Free me from this body of death
Come set this captive free
Come to me now, Lord Jesus, as I call upon your Name
Since your blood has washed and cleansed me
No, I'll never be the same
Worthy are you to be praised
Yes, praise your Holy Name
Oh, precious blood of Jesus, fill my heart with Joy and love
Through your Holy Spirit, Lord, revive me from above
Let your Joy spill over till my cup it overflows
Let your blessings rain from heaven
Through your great eternal love
Oh, blessed Holy Spirit
Here I am at your command
I won't be afraid though the storm clouds rage
Nor the dashing waves of life's demands
I'm sanctified through my savior's blood
And I'm ever protected by the Master's hands

I Believe It

When he said, "Ye must be born again"
I believe it
When he said, "The spirit will descend"
I believe it
The only way to heaven is through God's only Son
It's through his death on the cross
Down there, my victory's won
He said he arose from the dead
And I believe it
When they said he walked on water
I believe it
When he raised Lazarus from the dead
Fed five thousand with five loaves of bread
There the hungry that day was fed
I believe it
When he commanded the devils to flee
Opened the blinded eyes to see
He gave his life to set me free
I believe it
He said the earth will burn with fervent heat
I believe it
He said he's coming back to claim his own
And I believe it
He said that heaven would be my home
And he'll never leave me down here alone
When he said he's coming back
I believe it
What he said his Word is true
He's coming back for his chosen few
What he said in his Word is true
And I believe it

I Didn't Get It from Man

Chorus
I didn't get from man; I didn't get from man
This love I got down in my soul
I didn't get from man; bless my soul salvation's free
And I didn't get it from man, and man can't take it away from me

Verse 1
Jesus died at Calvary; he paid the price for me
Jesus died at Calvary; he paid the price for me
Jesus died at Calvary; he paid the price for me
And man can't take that away from me

Verse 2
Buy the truth and sell it not; that's what the Bible says
Buy the truth and sell it not; that's what the Bible says
Buy the truth and sell it not; that's what the Bible says
And the truth will set you free
(Repeat chorus)

Verse 3
I can worship in spirit and truth
That's what the Bible says
I can worship in spirit and truth
That's what the Bible says
I can worship in spirit and truth
That's what the bible says
And man can't take that away from me
(Repeat chorus)

Glory-bound Train

Chorus
Get on board, lost children
Get on board, lost children
Get on board, lost children
Will you ride that glory-bound train?

Verse 1
Just like so many others
From that narrow path I strayed
I went so far down life's wide road
I fear I'd lost my way
I met a man called Jesus
I talked with him today
He said, "My child, I know you're lost
"Come follow me. I know the way"
(Repeat two times) Chorus

Verse 2
There's a train that's bound for glory land
No fare for you to pay
I purchased your ticket with my blood
One day at Calvary
The train now is waiting
To take you home for free
No ticket fare is needed
Please get on board with me
(Chorus)

Verse 3
When we enter the gates of glory land
God's face, we'll surely see
He sent me here to take you home
Please get on board with me

Get on board, lost children
Get on board, lost children
Get on board, lost children
Let's ride that glory-bound train
(Repeat two times)

It Was There

Chorus
It was there at the cross I met Jesus
It was there my sin debt was paid
When I fell to my knees at the foot of the cross
It was there his precious blood poured over me

Dark was that day at Calvary's hill
Dark as the sin that covered me
But the veil it was rent; the lamb he was sent
So the face of my God I may see

It was there at the cross I met Jesus
It was there my sin debt was paid
When I fell to my knees at the foot of the cross
It was there his precious blood poured over me

Three days in the earth, my Savior did go
And took the keys out of old Satan's hands
Death, hell, and the grave held me captive, you see
(But Jesus unlocked that old door for me)

Repeat
It was there at the depths of my yearning soul
Sin and despair lay over me
Then I fell to my knees at my Savior's feet
It was there his mercy covered me

Chorus
The light of the Lamb shown so bright that day
So bright the light I did see
His living water flowed to the depths of my soul
As he cast all my sins to the sea

My Only Son

He's my only son, my only son
Dear, Lord, you know what that means
He's the joy of my life, a star in my eyes
He sure fills my world,
It's hard to believe
That my life's so complete,
'Cause he's here with me
What a treasure he's become,
Dear, Lord, he's my only son
"Little league baseball," I can still hear him say
"Daddy, will you practice with me?"
Game time is near, and I'll be there to cheer,
'Cause I know he's depending on me
He looks to the bleachers; I call out his name,
My heart pounds as he takes his swing,
The ball goes flying and there's no use denying that,
I'm as proud as any Daddy could be.
We're not together, his mommy and me
And that really hurts him; it's plain to see.
He won't leave my sight whenever I'm there,
He's Daddy's little boy, and, oh, how he cares.
I bought a pocket watch just the other day,
And he had to have one just the same way.
When I buy boots, you better believe.
He'll have to have some, just like me.
He's my only son; he's my only son,
Dear, Lord, you know what that means; he's the joy of my life,
A star in my eyes; he sure fills my world,
It's hard to believe; my life's so complete 'cause he's here with me.
Dear, Lord, he's my only son, yes Lord,
He's my only son.

Grandma's Cookie Jar

I love to visit my grandma
She always greets me with a kiss
She hugs me ever so gently
Are all grandmas like this?
Well, mine is very special
She has a cookie jar, you know
It looks just like a little bear
With a little blue coat
And lots of pink hair
I stick my hand inside
And find the cookies there
She always puts them in that jar
With lots of love and tender care
She always seems to know what kind
How does Grandma read my mind?
She bathes me when I go to bed
We share a lot when prayers are said
She tells me Jesus is my friend
And he'll always be right here with me
Till my life on earth it ends
God take good care of my grandma
I love her a lot, you see
She gives me hugs and kisses
And I know that my grandma loves me
Sometimes she picks me up from school
When Mommy's busy, that's the rule
But that's okay with me, you see
'Cause my grandma is cool
"I love you, Grandma"

The Great Commission

Verse 1
Go ye into all the world and preach the gospel
to every creature, He that believeth and is baptized
shall be saved; but he that believeth not shall be
damned. And these signs shall follow them that
believe. In my name shall they cast out devils
they shall speak with new tongues
they shall take up serpents and if they drink
any deadly thing it shall not hurt them
they shall lay hands on the sick and they
shall recover.

Verse 2
There is a Shepherd that gave a commission
many years ago; he bade us go out into the world
and bring in the sheep that he loves so
he said; many are called but few are chosen
the harvest is ripe but the laborers are few
will you be one to reap the harvest
yes, I will go, how about you?

Verse 3
So long we've been waiting for our call to glory
our feet has trodden on this barren land
through troubles and trials temptations and
sorrows
our cross grows heavy but it's part of the plan.

Verse 4
We'll keep pressing on no matter the cost
we're here on a mission to bring in the lost
there's not much time to tell people about Jesus
not much time now left here to choose
the Spirit is drawing won't you please answer
people, there's a heaven to gain and a hell to lose.

Verse 5
It won't be long till we hear that trumpet
the signs of the times are everywhere
look up, look up now don't be discouraged
the Lord's coming back his promise is clear
look up, look up, our waiting is over
look up, look up, our redemption is near.

Come see the Lamb

Chorus
Oh, come see the Lamb
Come, touch his nail-scarred hands
Look into the eyes of the sacrificial Lamb
His blood, it stained that old rugged cross
That was meant for you and me
He died to set us free
Oh, come see the Lamb

Verse 1
I stood there for a moment
Tears streaming down my face
Why would someone love me so much?
So much he'd die there in my place
The whip that stung his flesh that day
To many stripes my sin debt he paid
The crown of thorns upon his head
The blood-soaked robe lay on the ground
It was stained a crimson red
(Chorus)

Verse 2
My sins were blacker than the sky that day
But the Lord of creation took them all away
While yet his body was bleeding
Hanging there on the cross
"Father, forgive them" was his cry
He was pleading for the lost

Verse 3
What show of compassion what mercy what grace?
Why would Jesus die on the cross?
Just to take my place

Love is the only answer love is all I see
Love is the only reason I know
That he died there for you and me
(Chorus)

Send Down Your Blessing, Lord

Chorus
Send down your blessings, Lord
Let your mercy cover me
Lest I see no room for hope
And my life it flee from me
Send down your blessings, Lord
Let your mercy cover me

Verse 1
In my quest to enter your gates
Encounters I'll surely find
Stumbling blocks along the way
So many things that numb my mind
But I'm reminded of long ago
Of a Savior who was tried like me
Who gave his life that I may live
Upon a cruel tree
(Repeat chorus)

Verse 2
I raise my hands toward heaven
My anguished soul cries out to thee
Don't leave me here in this sin sick world
My Lord, my Savior, come rescue me
(Repeat chorus)

Verse 3
I have cast my burdens upon thee
As thou has commanded me to do
The Holy Spirit is my strength
And by his power, I'll make it through

So I give it all to thee; Lord, I commit it to your hands
Can't hang on to nothing here because nothing here will
stand
(Repeat chorus)
Send down your blessings, Lord
Holy Spirit, dwell in me

Lazarus Come Forth

"Lazarus, come forth," the master has spoken
"Take off the grave clothes that had you bound
"For so long"
"Lazarus, come forth. Don't stay in that grave now"
The master has spoken, "Lazarus, come forth"
Sickness has stricken my life and my family
It seemed that death had compassed me all around
When all of the faith I had seem to vanish
I heard his voice call me from depths of my soul
"Lazarus, come forth. Your sickness is defeated
"I conquered death at Calvary's hill
"Come, hear my voice that has spoken life to you
"By faith, you are loosed now, Lazarus, come forth"
I'm tired and I'm weary so long I have suffered
Pain and misery has taken hold of my life
From these tear-filled eyes, Lord, my voice cries out to you
Just speak to this body
And I'll be made alive
Then Martha stepped up and said to the Master
"Whom thou loveth is sick and may die"
Jesus said, "Martha, did I not say unto thee
"If thou wouldest believe
"You'll see the glory of God"
When the Master called my name, the grave could not hold me
I'm following the One who gave his life for me
Hallelujah, praise God I'm loosed from this prison
The Master, he spoke
Now thank God I am free
I am alive

Why Are You Running?

Chorus
My child, why are you running?
Why are you running from me?
A long time ago, I called you
Your face, I clearly did see
Your life, I spared from the storm that seized you
I rescued you from life's raging sea
So when you are weary from all of your running
My child, please run home to me

Verse 1
Why did you leave your Father's house?
To travel the road of sin
This road you're on is filled with heartache and sorrow
No peace will you find within
There's always something on this road
To snare your soul from me
The pride of life the lust of the flesh
It's all your eyes will ever see

Verse 2
On this road, there's always temptation
Death and hell are everywhere
Open your eyes; don't stay in the darkness
Open your eyes and run home to me
Out there, you'll thirst for that life-giving water
But no life-giving water will there be
No safety net from the lies of the spoiler
That took your soul so far from me
(Chorus)

Verse 3
Come home where the light burns brightly for you
Haven't you wallowed in the hog pen too long?
You've eaten of the husk
Where the hogs, they did eat
When there's plenty of food here at home
My child, I'm patiently waiting on you
Your sweet face I long to see
I'll kill the fatted calf
Put on your back the finest robe
A gold ring on your finger there'll be
(Chorus)

The Master's Aboard

Lord, I know you're watching every move that I make,
I cannot hide all of my mistakes.
My sins are open to your eyes;
I know you'll correct my foolish lies.
This house of flesh that I'm groaning in,
Will someday soon, the victory win.
I was poor wretched and miserable.
Then you spoke my name, and Lord,
Since that day, I've not been the same.
So I'll be content to live in this house,
I won't try to hide nor turn it about—
After all, Lord, when you went away,
You left me a help mate to guide me each day.
The sweet Holy Spirit will ever abide,
In this house of mine to lovingly guide.
So why should I fear the storms that arise?
The Master's aboard; it's peaceful inside.
We're not really promised there won't be some pain,
But we know through it all, there's a heaven to gain.
No life isn't easy,
Just take it one day at a time.
For yet just a little while, we'll be home,
With him, yes, my child, in the sweet by and by.

Lord, Speak to Me

Lord, speak to me; I'm here all alone
Please speak to me, Lord
Oh, where have you gone?
I'm cold and I'm bitter, but what can I do?
There's no one to guide me, oh, Lord, I need you
I long to call upon your name
But I feel so unworthy, Lord
I'm drowning in shame
Come, touch this heart that's turned to stone
Just say the word, Lord
And it will be gone
Too many nights, I've tossed, and I've turned
Come touch me now, Lord
I know I can learn
I've opened my heart; I've said all I can
Now for the rest, Lord, I leave in your hands
Don't scold me in your anger; I'm only a man
I know you can help me, Lord
'Cause I've done all I can

I'm Gonna Climb That Mountain

Chorus
I'm gonna climb that mountain, Lord
I'm gonna sail life's sea
I'm gonna lift your name on high
Down here upon my knees
When that mountain show's itself
I won't have far to reach
'Cause I'm gonna climb that mountain, Lord
Down here upon my knees

Verse 1
There's troubles and trials on every hand
These mountains seem so high
But when I'm faced down here with them
No, I won't run and hide
I'll just go down on my knees
With you right by my side
At your command, they'll flee away
Oh, Lord, you are my guide
I'm gonna climb that mountain, Lord
Yes, I'm gonna sail life's sea
I'm gonna lift your name on high
Down here upon my knees
When that mountain shows itself

I won't have far to reach
'Cause I'm gonna climb that mountain, Lord
Down here upon my knees

Verse 2
So devil, you just go ahead and build those mountains high
Those walls you're building around this child
Will crumble by and by
God promised me the victory here
And I won't run and hide
At your command, they'll flee away
Oh, Lord, you are my guide

Chorus
I'm gonna climb that mountain, Lord
I'm gonna sail life's sea
I'm gonna lift your name on high
Down here upon my knees
When that mountain shows itself
I won't have far to reach
'Cause I'm gonna climb that mountain, Lord
Down here upon my knees
Yes, I'm gonna climb that mountain, Lord
Down here upon my knees

Lord I'm Waiting on You

Lord, I'm waiting on you
Yes, Lord, I'm waiting on you
You said someday that you'd return
To take me to Canaan's fair land
Lord, I'm waiting on you
Oh, Lord, I'm waiting on you
I want to be there to walk streets of gold
Yes, Lord, I'm waiting on you
I can't wait till that day, till I hear that trumpet
And you split that eastern sky
I'll leave this old earth in a shout of Glory
Lord, I'm waiting on you
When my feet leaves the ground, I won't turn around
I'll bid this world goodbye
I'm headed for my home way up in the sky
Lord, I'm waiting on you
Yes, I'll be there in the twinkling of an eye
Oh, Lord, I'm waiting on you
When I see the river that John spoke of
I'll sit down by Jesus's side
We'll talk of the love that got me to Glory
And no tears will dim my eyes
I'll see his sweet face, hear the angel's holy cry
As my feet walk on streets paved with gold
I'm headed for home, oh, won't you come along?
Oh, Lord, I'm waiting on you
Yes, Lord, I'm waiting on you

Let Us Be Your Servants, Lord

Let us be your servants, Lord
Yes, let us stand the test
When we are on the road for you
Lord, let us do our best

Chorus
Our hearts are set to follow you
Wherever you may lead
Whether it's to sink or swim
Or whether it's to bleed
So here we are, your servants, Lord
Come, show us what to do
We're marching up to Zion's hill
We'll do it all for you
Our hearts are set to follow you
Wherever you may lead
Whether it's to sink or swim
Or whether it's to bleed
And by your grace
We'll be there, Lord
Wherever there's a need
Yes, and by your grace, we'll be there, Lord
Wherever there's a need

Forgiveness

How much do I love thee?

I want to know this man from Galilee
Who stretched out his arms and died for me
"How much do I love thee?" I heard him say
Then he stretched out his arms and was crucified
that way
We go about our merry way
And, yes, people, we think that we're okay
We go to church and that's not wrong for in the church
Christians belong, but let's not forget
What we're going for to fellowship and love
For strength and joy the building it serves
The people who congregate
Its purpose is no more than, it's fate
So who are we to say who can come in or who can't?
The sinner is welcome just like the saint
For if we exclude those who are in need
Who will touch their lives? Who will plant the seeds?
So wake up, people, before it's too late
If the sinner's not welcome, what is our fate?
It's he who shed his blood, not us
So why should we argue?
Why should we fuss?
So grab ahold of the hand of the one going astray
Grab ahold and love him love him today

Forgiveness

How much do I love thee?

If he sins against us/ We must forgive/
Just like Jesus/ Who died on the hill/
They slapped him/ They mocked him/
They beat him and more/
They did this until/ The blood did pour/
They placed a crown of thorns/ Upon his head/
Till his blood did flow/a crimson red/
Blood and water flowed from his side that day/
Oh, we ask why it had to be this way/
It was an example/For us to see/How much he loved/
You and me/ They did those things to him/ But he forgave/
It's not hate/ That hung him on the tree/
Oh, no, but it was love/ For you and me/
But not only for us/ Did he pay that cost/
But also for the other ones/ That's lost/
So if their lost/ Lets take them by the hand/
And gently pull on their heart strings/ For their soul we may win/
Let's not cast them aside/
As many people do/ and say they love Jesus/
Oh, how can this be true?/
If we say we love Jesus/ We don't turn them away/
For if his Spirit is in us/ he doesn't work that way/

Forgiveness

How much do I love thee?

Let's sit down and talk awhile/ You and I / and
examine and see/ If his Spirit's inside/
If he's really in us of a truth/ we won't have a
problem of forgiving people/ of what they do/
We'll love them until/ their sin goes away/ For that's
what Jesus did/ On that day/
When he said/ I came to seek that/ Which was lost/
He knew too well/ There would be cost/ This life's
not easy/ It's full of sin/ So count the cost/ Before
you begin/ It's Jesus who died/ and bore the shame,
So we must forgive them/ If we bare his name/
So when I'm reminded/ of other people's sins/ I go back
to the day/ When it all began/ The day I met Jesus/
And he took me by the hand/ He wiped away my tears
And forgive me of my sins/ He pulled on my heart
strings/ Ever so gently with love/ He wrote my
Name/ in the Lambs book of life/ And he sealed
it with his blood/
So hear these words and heed them well/
For the greatest love story/ they do tell
"Father, forgive them for they know not what they do"
So, Christians, we must be that way. If someone sins against you, just look at the
cross and what they did to Jesus because they were lost. And he said:
"Father, forgive them, for they no not what they do"
So if his Spirit is in you of a truth, you'll also know
"They know not what they do"

Let Me Be the Rock

Upon this rock, I will build my church
And the gates of hell shall not prevail against it

Chorus
Lord let me be the rock where you build your church
Lord let it stand even through the worst
Sanctified and true standing just for you
Lord, let me be the rock
Yes, let me be the rock
And when you ask this question, Lord,
"Whom do men say that I, the son of man, am?"
Then let me and all who know you reply
"Thou art the Christ, the son of the living God"
And as he told his disciple Peter
May we also hear
"Blessed art thou for flesh and blood
"Hath not revealed it unto thee
"But my Father which is in heaven"
Lord, let me be the rock where you build your church
Lord, let it stand even through the worst
Sanctified and true standing just for you
Lord, let me be the rock
Yes, let me be the rock
And as he said to his disciple Peter

May we also hear
"And I will give unto thee the keys to the Kingdom
"Of heaven, and whatsoever thou shalt
"Bind on earth shall be bound in Heaven
"And whatsoever thou shalt loose on earth
"Shalt be loosed in Heaven
"If any Man shall come after me, let
"Him deny himself and take up his cross
"And follow me"
Lord, let me be the rock where you build
Your church, Lord, let it stand
Even through the worst
Sanctified and true standing just for you
Let me be the rock, Lord, let me be the rock
Yes, let me be the rock

Visions I've Had

The following three pages are dreams and visions I had. I lived in Murray, Kentucky, at the time. This was printed in our local newspaper there.

To know me is of no importance; but to know what I'm about to tell you is everything. Everywhere I go, I see signs saying, "God Bless America." And it' so true. We want the blessings of God upon our nation, but there are conditions on getting these blessings. In 1 Chronicles 7:14, 19–22, you may say he was talking to Solomon. God is the same God; he never changes. He's the same yesterday, today, and forever neither does his Son, Jesus Christ, of whom these words are spoken about in Hebrews 13:8.

What I want to tell you about are visions I have which, I believe, are warnings to us and our nation concerning the end times. I don't know about you, but I feel it greatly. And I feel these visions has significance. This is the way I had them and in this order.

I was standing on the ground. I looked up, and the sky was darkened. And the clouds were rolling, and I could hear a great rumbling as they started to part and clear. A great big *M* appeared in the sky. And what was put in my mind and impressed upon my heart was the *Great Messiah* like it was impressed upon me to be prepared for his coming which, I believe, the horns should be blowing, announcing his arrival.

Again, I was standing on the ground. I saw a cloud forming. It was rolling. I stood looking in amazement as it started toward me. It was low over my head.

I watched as it came closer. The cloud began to take the shape of humanlike forms. The sound was like that of stampeding cattle. These forms were like mist of clouds, but you could tell they were human forms. As they came closer, I could see sheer panic on their faces. Their eyes looked like black holes, and their mouths were also like black holes that were wide open with screams, practically running over each other from the fear of whatever they were fleeing from (Revelation 6:12–17).

It was almost like the Exodus. A great multitude stood before me like they were waiting instructions on what to do. There were men, women, and children—so many I couldn't count them. They would become noisy, and when they did, I would lift my hand way above my head and make a motion like a cut-off motion. And the crowd, even down to the children, would become dead silent, as though the crowd was subject to my every command. This one somewhat bothers me. I want to follow the Lord's leading in my life, but I don't want to think of myself as above anyone. The Lord knows what this is all about, and someone has to take lead as Moses and Joshua did and tell the people what's about to take place and to *warn* them.

God has been patient for over two thousand years, giving people space to repent and turn to him. That's why he's still waiting. But people, I believe in my heart he's sending people to tell you to repent and to get prepared for that great and noble day of the Lord. I am his servant and want to be subject to his will. That's why I'm taking time to tell you this. Heed the warning signs. Turn to him. If you don't know him, get to know him.

"Seek and ye shall find, knock and the door shall be opened unto you" (Mathew 7:7–8). God loves you. It's not his will for anyone to perish. So please, dear loved ones, seek after his Face. He's waiting for you, and he's waiting on you. That's why he's put off his coming back for so long. He's giving you space to repent and to seek him.

Don't wait too late. I've told you. I've done what he's commanded me to do. Please consider yourselves warned. Don't put it off. Don't be one of those in my vision who were running for their lives. But be one of those who repent, and you won't have anything to fear upon his returning. God loves you, and I love you.

(Read Revelation 7, The Great Multitude).

—Martha Geary

Repent

The world as we know it
Will soon be gone
Mankind is going somewhere
Heaven or hell for eternity
The choice is very clear
So won't you be ready when Jesus comes?
Dear friend, our fate is drawing near
So lift up your voice to Jesus today
Repent, and he will hear
Like a mighty rushing wind
The Spirit will descend
Jesus, oh, Jesus will save your precious soul
Rivers of water will pour over you
Cleansing every sin, washing you clean
And making you whiter than snow
Don't know about you
But my choice is clear
With Jesus I want to go
Down on my knees is where I found my Savior
A long, long time ago

Has Anybody Seen My Daughter?

To Deanna

Has anybody seen my daughter?
I've been searching for her everywhere
I think life has swallowed her up
I believe life's adder has bitten her
She's become numb, numb from the bite
Oh, Lord, won't you teach her how to fight?
She used to be so lovely, so kind
Her beautiful heart longed for her mother
Her little hand was always in mine
Oh, how she loved her mother
Has anybody seen my daughter?
She has dark blonde hair
And her eyes are green like mine
She couldn't even stand to be
Out of my sight
Oh, where has she gone?
I miss her so
Has anybody seen my daughter?
Could it be someone has taken her
Far from me?
Could it be someone has told her
I'm not needed anymore?
That I'm only someone in her past
Only a memory that shouldn't last
I would offer a reward
But Jesus already paid it
Her price is far above rubies
She is her mother's precious jewel
And her Father in heavens
Special daughter
Her love was mine; was it only for a time?
Has anybody seen my daughter?

If per chance you see her passing by
Would you tell her where I am? I'm here
Maybe she doesn't know I'm still here
Right where she left me
Maybe life has swallowed her up
Maybe she has drank
From life's bitter cup
The adder of life has bitten her
And she's numb from the bite
Lord, teach her how to fight
Has anybody seen my daughter?
She will come back, I know it
My love will bring her back
From where she's at
This dark and lonely place
That's kept her from me
The light will shine through
Cause a mother's love is strong
Even the chains of death can't hold it
God himself will break the chains
They were never meant to be
He will set my daughter free
Because the bond is strong
Between her and me
Her lovely face once again I'll see

Love,
Mom

Our Son

For John & Vicki

Jamie our son
We shall never forget your sweet face
Nor the warm greeting of your loving embrace
The glow of your smile
Oh, how it could brighten our day
You touched so many lives
In your own special way
Sleep peacefully, my child, and take your rest
'Cause knowing you here on this earth
So many lives down here you blessed
If there was a need, you were always there
To calm a heart or dry a tear
God saw it all. He knew you well
So many good stories your friends did tell
We miss you, son; our hearts still break
But our God sees all, and he makes no mistakes
What a home our child God prepared for you
The streets are made of pure gold
Nothing on earth can compare to it
The half has never been told
Our lives down here are empty now
Since you went away
But someday, we'll walk those streets of gold
With you, son
Together some sweet day

Dustin

I was told that you are not doing well,
I hope that you don't mind that I was told.
This is nothing to be ashamed of;
You lost a brother
That is really something in your life
It's tough to deal with.
I am your grandmother, and even though
I haven't been with you kids a lot, you've been
In this family many years and believe it or not,
I do love you all and care what happens to each of you.
Jamie leaving this world knocked me off my feet.
Even though death is nothing new to me. I've lost
my dad, my mom, grandparents, sisters, and a brother.
A nephew that was only seventeen years old.
Aunts and uncles, the list goes on. "Death is no stranger to me."
But my mom's death cut me deep. I had a nervous
breakdown. Deanna was born three weeks after Mom
died. A birth is something hard for a woman to
contend with in itself, much less, having to deal
with the death of a parent.
I'm sharing this with you for a reason, and I
Hope you don't mind.
My life has been a hurtful thing but with each
tragedy I clung tightly to my Lord; he has been
my best friend. He's what's kept me sane
In an insane world of hurt and loss.
I hang on to him with every fiber of my being,
I'm his most dependent child. Every time something
Happens, no matter what it is—good, bad, or ugly
He's always there, lifting me up, drying my tears,
giving me peace of mind, and taking away and calming my fears.
This is how our Lord works in our lives
when we learn to trust and turn to him.

He made us a promise: "The ones who trust him"
that he'd never leave us nor forsake us. And
believe me trust me on this: he doesn't
No matter what happens to me on this old earth
I'll always cling tight to my Lord. When I look
back on my life, I realize he's always been
there, and I know for sure till my life ends
He always will be. Our Father in heaven doesn't
lie. When he makes a promise, you can take it to the bank.
I challenge you, Dustin. Lay all your worries,
Your illness, your fears, all the things that's
causing the storm inside you; he will take all
of it and calm your storms and give you a peace
that surpasses all understanding. Trust me,
I'm one who knows. I've been where you're at.
He did it for me, and he'll do it for you.
Read your Bible. The Lord wants you to know him
Seek his face diligently; I was like Jacob I told
him I wasn't going to. Let go till he blessed me.
And he did. And he hasn't stopped.
I love him because he first loved me. He's my heavenly
Daddy. My earthly daddy is gone. But God won't ever
leave me till he takes me home to be with him forever.
I don't have to be afraid anymore 'cause Jesus
conquered death, hell, and the grave for me; and if
I don't have to fear those three things anymore,
What else is there left to fear? I'm not going to hell
'Cause Jesus saved my soul, the grave can't hold me down
'Cause Jesus arose the third day. And death will only
Take me home to live forever. This all comes with
trusting Jesus for what he did at Calvary. He paid our
sin debt. Thank God I'm free!
I Love You, Dustin

—Your Grandma

The Phone Call

Hello, is anybody there?
Hello, I need to hear your voice
This is your child, Lord
Please answer; hello, can you hear me?
I've been waiting for so long, Lord
Just about to give up
Been in this gutter so long
Don't even know how to look up
Hello, can anybody hear me?
I've just spent my last dime
Haven't had anything to eat now
It's been such a long, long time
I'm cold and alone so far from home
Hello, Lord, are you on the phone?
Can't seem to sleep my body's trembling and weak
Afraid to close my eyes
Darkness and fear in every corner
Evil stands on every side
Hello, oh, Lord, I knew you would answer when I called
I knew you'd never leave me nor forsake me
No, never at all
Hello, child, here I am I've been waiting for you to call me
My child, how I love you
How I love you, can't you see?
Your life is so special
So special, child, to me
The very hairs of your head are numbered
I sent my Son to die in your stead
I sent the stars to shine for you I will give you daily bread
What more can I do to prove I love you?
Ask and I'll give it to thee
Nothing can soar as high as my love
Ask and you will receive

I'll bow the Heavens I'll come down to you
Upon a cherub I will fly
Child, I'll thunder in the Heavens
I'll send you rainbows by and by
Ask, my child, if you need wisdom
It's my pleasure to give it to thee
Ask, my child, if you need understanding
For without it, where would you be?
Ask, my child, if you need love
For love is who I am
I will surely give it to you
It's on my Word you can depend
Oh how long, child, I've been waiting
Just to hear you call on me
It's my pleasure to give you the kingdom
Just ask, and you will receive

For Dustin with Love
From Jesus and Grandma

This was written especially
for you.

If I Could Leave You Anything, I'd Leave You Jesus

For my children

Children, come close and listen while you can
Life is but a vapor down here
So let me tell you about this man
I learned of him long ago
Sitting on momma's knee
Oh, how her eyes would shine so brightly
Speaking of him to me
She told me about the things he'd done
How he died upon a tree
How he came to this old world
To save a child like me
She said I need to tell you of him
Cause someday. He'll call me Home
I won't be here to guide your life
So it's in his mighty hands
Your lives to Jesus I leave
If I could leave you anything, I'd leave you Jesus
He's the only one who can lead you
Safely back home someday to me
When my eyes down here have at last grown dim
And my life I've lived on earth for him
My Bible lying by my side
And its words have been my daily guide
When I take my final ride
If I could leave you anything
I'd leave you Jesus
For he has been my rock
He has been my daily bread
He has been my source of comfort
By his spirit, I was fed

When I was weary and heavy laden
When no friend on earth I could find
When everyone here they did forsake me
Only his love was my peace of mind
So if I could leave you anything
I'd leave you Jesus
When all others forsake you
He'll be by your side
His arms alone will guide and protect you
Till you take your heavenly flight
My children, all my earthly possessions
I leave to you
But most of all
I leave you Jesus

True Love Is

True Love is loving
Even when Love is not returned
True Love is unconditional
It doesn't say, "I'll love you if"
It says, "I'll love you in spite of"
True Love is not always finding fault in others
It looks over the faults in others
And always tries to find the good
True Love is holding our tongue
True love does not spread gossip about others even when they are saying wrong things about us
True Love is being there when were needed wherever there is a need; Love says, fill it
True Love is saying in any given situation, "What would Jesus do? How would Jesus react?
True Love is giving (charity) of yourself until it hurts, not holding back good from others
Give, give, give not only of money; tithing is also giving of your time, giving of your efforts to someone, to worthy causes to help the poor, the needy, or just to be a friend when a friend is needed.
Love others as Christ loved us.

(Luke 23:34)

Our Family

A family is a sacred thing
Ordained from God above
He created it for our pleasure
So we would have someone to love
Family is connection,
Brothers and sisters, Mom and Dad
In this realm, there's always someone
Lifting you up and making you glad
When you're down, there's words of kindness
When you're sick, there's a helping hand
Through a family, God has shown
His infinite love to mortal man
In our family, there were quite a few
Mom and Dad did not believe in birth control
The Bible clearly states;
It's he who opens or closes the womb
So they took that to mean,
God knows what he's doing
So there were eleven of us children
Oh, we were looked down on quite a bit,
But my mom and dad did not care
Ultimately; God was going to have his way,
Not man.
Our dad was fire; our mother was water
Yes, we got the best of both worlds
joined together to become one. The
strength of God was the center of that world
when it became one spiritually, physically, and mentally.
Through struggles, trials, temptations,
through floods, storms, reproaches,
through life and death, pain and sorrow,
our large family that was created
from God above; still stands strong today.

God was the center of that home,
Dad and Mom knew where their strength
had to be, in order for us to survive.
So they nurtured and cherished, God's love
and instilled that in us.
As children, we didn't have much
Outside our family, but that only served,
to make our family ties stronger
We loved, we laughed; at times, we cried,
but we were always there for each other.
I'm sure we all had questions at the time.
Our Dad who was a strict disciplinarian,
raised us with a Bible in one hand and
a razor strap in the other.
All of us wondered why we had to be
so harshly whipped with that old strap.
But the Bible clearly states;
A rod is for the fool's back, and foolishness
is bound in the heart of a child,
But the rod of correction will absolutely
take it out.
If you don't do wrong, you don't get whipped.
How hard is that to understand?
Needless to say, it surely didn't take us
Children long to understand that concept.
When we grew up and had children
of our own the truth of discipline became
Very apparent.
We look on our Dad with respect
and admiration.
And, Mom, the meek little woman who
knew what love was all about, who
calmed our fears and kissed away

our hurts and bruises.
Who was meek but possessed an inner
strength that could only have come
from having a personal relationship
with our heavenly Father.
Our family will remain strong and
Connected and will be there to give
a kind word when needed to each other;
It will stand because it was built
On that rock, which is Christ our Savior.
This is how we are supposed to behave
in our own families and also toward our
brothers and sisters in Christ
whoever they may be.
My brother and sister;
We have lost our dad & mom
four brothers, four sisters, they have
gone on before us.
But we have this hope that was instilled
in us from them; we'll meet again in
a better place—in a land where
We'll never die.
This is our promise from our heavenly Father
This is our hope of eternal life
This is what we will pass on to our children
My family, I love you!
Your Sis,
Martha

The Family Album

Believe, Dream, Will…
And place it in the Hands of God.

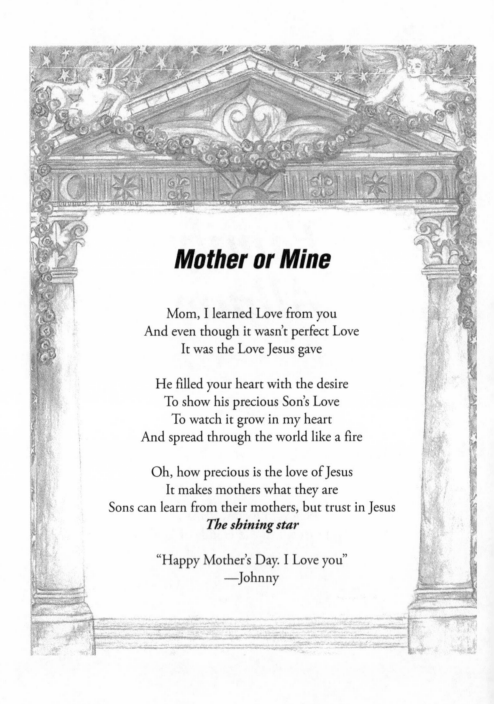

Mother or Mine

Mom, I learned Love from you
And even though it wasn't perfect Love
It was the Love Jesus gave

He filled your heart with the desire
To show his precious Son's Love
To watch it grow in my heart
And spread through the world like a fire

Oh, how precious is the love of Jesus
It makes mothers what they are
Sons can learn from their mothers, but trust in Jesus
The shining star

"Happy Mother's Day. I Love you"
—Johnny

Deborah Lynn McStoots,
my daughter

Momma's girl

Precious Memories

God blessed me with some beautiful
children, not only looks but also in *heart*.
Thank you, my Father in heaven

Jack, Debbie's husband

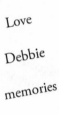 Love

Debbie

memories

Love

Jack

memories

Forever

Jack & Lealand—Lee, Lee   Jack & Debbie

Jack & Debbie   Debbie

Lee, Lee

Lee, Lee

Ayden & Debbie

Jack

Jack & Ayden—Blue's Brothers   Ayden

Debbie, Lee, Lee and Ayden.
Oh, how cute is this?

Ayden

Lealand

Lealand & Ayden

Debbie

Debbie when she was young

My Debbie at 2 1/2 years of age. A doll holding a doll.

Ayden Wyatt Debbie's little Man

Ayden Wyatt Debbie's little Man

John, Debbie, Deanna, Shaun

Jack

Love that Hug! Mom & Debbie

(Left to right: John, Debbie, Martha, Deanna, David)

Momma's four sweethearts

Precious Memories

School
Day
Memories

Mommy's
Memories

My Johnny at six years old.
Look at that smile! Wouldn't
that melt your heart?

John

This is my Johnny at the age of six years old.

I asked him, "John, is there anything you'd like to contribute to my book?"

He said, "Yes, Mom. I'd like for you to include that picture of me with my teeth missing in front."

Only my John would make this request. That's what makes him so special. And I will honor it. I can say one thing that truly makes him so dear in his mother's eyes. He's a Christian. He lives in Florida, and I don't get to see him often, and I do miss him so. But we still have our talks via telephone. He is the one who lit the torch that sparked the flame in me for this book. Thank you so very much, my heavenly Father, for blessing me with John. What a special son he is.

Alvin, Les, & Chasity

MY
Bradley
Grandmas
Baby

Brandon's
B-Day (left)
Me, Brandon
I'm Hugging
and sweet little
Bradley

Little Dave
& Johnny

Me
Buster,
Tayler,
and
Cody

John
&
Dave

Sheriff John G.
All better Be good!

John & Cousin Becky
Isn't this sweet?

Sweet Memories

John, a baby in mom's arms
Little Debbie on the porch
with uncle Roger.

The tiger's birthday blowing out his candles;
little Dave watching Steve standing by the
door; Sweet little Dave was wanting some
cake look at that face! Hurry, brother!

Memories

School Days
John was always a star in his mother's eyes.

Never Ending Story

Fifties fun at school
Johnny won *best-dressed* boy

JIM YOUNG - Senior
Halfback - Monster Back

JOHN GEARY - Senior
Halfback - Corner Back

Jim was Johnny's best friend all through school.

John & Jim
"John will always be my hero."
They were always together

John in his big man suit.
He thought something was funny.

Fifties fun

"HAPPY DAYS" was the theme of a special program at Grayson County Middle School Thursday afternoon. At least 100 students dressed in the style of the 1950s, and several took part in skits to entertain the other students. One of the highlights of the program was a performance by a "band" that pantomimed rock and roll hits from 15 to 20 years ago. While "vocalist" Sammy Montgomery, top photo, was doing "Splish Splash", John Marshall doused him with a bucket of water. Others in the band, from left, are Hank Egan, David Swift and James Heavrin. Above are winners of the costume contest: Lori Logsdon and James Heavrin, best couple, nearest jukebox; Jill Norris, left, best girl; and Johnny Geary, best boy.

Mike Lively tells the crowd that he is "The Fonz." Other cast members from left, are Lynette Saltsman, Tim Wilson, David Huff, Doris Oller, Steve Sanford, Jennifer White, Valerie Hayes and Tim Mudd. Above, even teachers got into the act, as librarian Shirley Wayne and math teacher Brenda Gibson did the jitterbug. The program was sponsored by the GCMS Student Council and grew out of a Fifties Dance held last year.

1980 Grayson County Cougar Football Team
John is #26 front row

Senior Captain
Steve Fulkerson, James Hunt, Ted Torrance, Bob Coulson

Grayson County Cougars Roster

Name	NO.	GR.	POS.
Richie Bryant	78	10	G/DE
Kevin Embry	63	10	G/T
Glen Stikeleather	14	10	QB/S
Alan Hatfield	88	11	HB/QB
Alan Tilford	52	11	C/NG
Ken Henderson	73	11	T
Jason Webb	74	11	T
Bob McCloud	75	11	T
Tony Grubbs	77	11	T
Jon Decker	32	11	FB/LB/K
Wayne Meredith	24	11	HB/CB
Dale Baldwin	45	11	HB/CB
Steve Givan	12	11	QB/K
Jon Harned	84	11	SE/QB/S
Jim Morris	36	11	FB/NG
Mike Pierce	80	11	SE/CB
Rick Webb	83	11	TE/MB
Mark O'neil	70	11	G/DE
Steve Fulkerson	62	12	G/LB
James Hunt	64	12	G/NG
Richard Alvey	82	12	TE/DE
Bob Coulson	51	12	C/DE
*John Geary	<u>26</u>	<u>12</u>	<u>HB/CB</u>
*Jim Young	<u>42</u>	<u>12</u>	<u>HB/MB</u>
Billy Thompson	43	9	HB/MB
Alfred Goldsberry	48	9	HB/S
Bobby Gaither	72	9	T/TE/DE/K
Todd Gallagher	87	9	TE/DE
Jim Scalf	11	9	SE/DB

Jim Johnson	33	9	HB/CB
Chris Vaugn	91	9	TE/DE
Clint Wallingford	53	9	T
Reid Hart	69	10	T
Sam McCloud	16	10	QB/LB
Scott Mccann	66	10	G/LB
Joey Wilson	50	10	C/NG
Mike Gallagher	68	10	G/LB
John Goff	30	10	FB/LB
Chuck Johnson	34	10	HB/CB
Albert Coleman	20	10	HB/CB
Dennis Thomas	81	10	SE/CB
Keith Minton	10	12	SE/CB
John Williams	22	12	SE/CB
Ted Torrance	86	12	HB/S
Jamie Palmer	76	12	T

My son Johnny Edward Geary

Johnny & Vicki on
their wedding day

Vickie

John

Memories

Sweet
Memories

Love

Love

with, Jamie, Dustin & Kristy

Johnny and Vicki
forever

God is on awesome God!
He is our Love.
He is our Forgiveness.
He is our Redeemer.
He is our Restorer.

Through him, we find hope and peace
for our present as well as our future.

NEVER ENDING STORY

The Gearys

Kristy & Jimmy's daughter
Kylie Reese—John &
Vicki's granddaughter

Christopher
John & Vicki's grandson
Kristy & Jimmy's son
John & Vicki

Jamie

Jimmy and Kristy live in Florida.
(Jimmy is a policeman.)

Jamie is deceased; he left this world
at only twenty-six years old.

Johnny & Vicki
Children:

Dustin
Kristy
Jamie

Dustin

Love You!

Miss You!

My sister Elaine You can see her Son, Eric on my son David's Wedding picture. Elaine has two more children: Michael and Dawn

Elaine

Elaine called me "Momma Sister" She stayed with me a lot of her life. I took care of her and Momma.

Memories

Memories

Elaine daughter Dawn and her Husband

Elaine's son Eric

Me, Eric, Elaine, Doris, Deanna, Shawn, singing in church

My David playing outside in his undies.
Don't you all laugh. He was cool. He didn't
care. He was having a good time. Momma's boy,
still is. If he were 80, he'd still be my baby!

"Mommas Special Memories"

Smile Sharon
God
Loves
you

Alpha,
Edith

Sharon House

How precious this
is my Grandbabies

Brandon, Bradley

Left to right
Betty,
Martha,
Debbie,
Deanna,
Shawn

Deanna
&
David—
Deanna's
wedding

Memories

Memories

David & Mom—Deanna's wedding

Me, modeling

David. Wasn't he so precious?

Tayler
Davis's son

Ty
Ty
Sweetheart

David Aaron Geary, my son
Graduation Day, proud mommy

Love
you
Cody

Looks like
Daddy;
David's son

Together Forever

David & Valarie their Wedding Day

Memories Forever

Cody and Tyler

Memories

Left to Right Martha, Val, David, Buster (center), Tim

Happy Times

Love

(Left to Right: Tabatha, Valarie, David, Eric, Elaine's son)

Little Miracle

Destini Rayne

David and Valarie's
Prize Possession
This is their only daughter. Of course,
the boys are their prizes also.

The Geary Family

Nathaniel William (Nate)

Destini Rayne
Our little sweet Destini

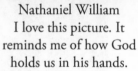

Nathaniel William
I love this picture. It
reminds me of how God
holds us in his hands.

Timothy (Tim)

David and Valarie's children

My beautiful Deanna

My little Deanna. How cute is this?
Those green eyes, that blonde hair.
Yep, I think she's a keeper.

Mommy's
Girl

Deanna Dawn

Momma Dee with Shawn & Brandon on the floor

Memories

Sweet
Memories

Peek-a-boo, Brandon

Love

Brandon & Shawn

Love

Fun
Memories

Memories

Love my grandbabies

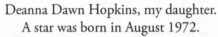

Deanna Dawn Hopkins, my daughter.
A star was born in August 1972.

Memories  Love

Deanna could have been a model. New York
called her. This mother did not want anything
to take her affections from her God. He's more
important than all the money in this world.

Keith & Deanna
Their Wedding Day

Timeless Beauty

Love

Forever

My Dee

My granddaughter was saying, "Come on."

Memories

Memories

Granny's
Girl

Sarah
Dawn

Love

Love

I love this picture.
Deanna's daughter, Sarah Dawn.

Tasha,
a jewel
of a girl

Tasha

Brandon
my quiet
one

Shawn my
loving one

Tim, also
my loving
one

Bradley,
grandmas
little
show off

Isn't he so
handsome?

From left to right:
Brandon, Shawn, Timmy and Bradley.

Grandmas
Memories

Are these all so very cute?

"Unforgetable"

Sweet Faces

My grandchildren.

Precious
Memories

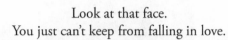

Look at that face.
You just can't keep from falling in love.

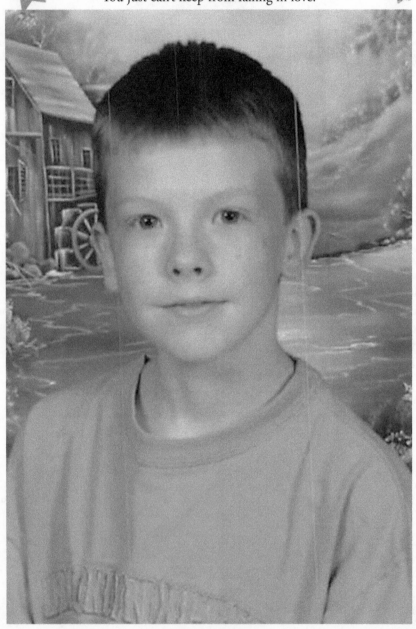

Shawn Michael

Sarah Dawn at seven. Quiet little charmer.

Precious
Memories

Grandmas
Buddy

Princess Sarah

Buster & Me

Me when I was working in private care for the elderly. The little thing I'm holding says it all to everyone!

I love you!

Susie

Childhood Buddies

The Crew
The Blanton Family

Three
not in
the
picture

Arcel
Cecil
Roger

The Geary Family

me again

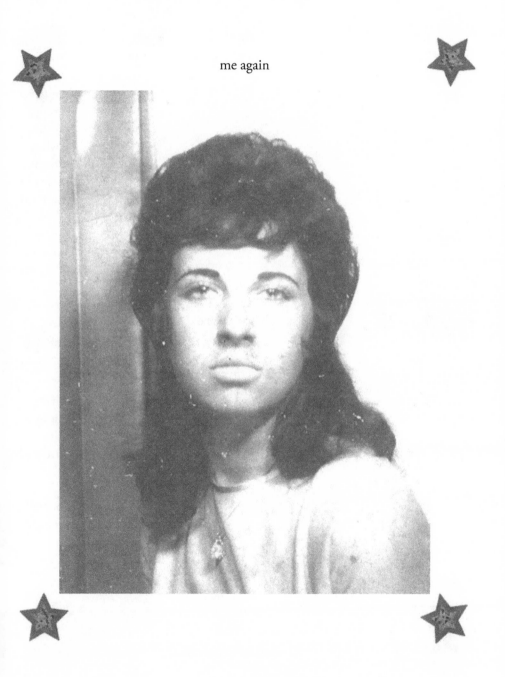

My Precious
Mom & Dad

You never fully realize what someone means to you until they're taken from you.

Mom and Dad
September 27, 1925
Dad was eighteen years old. Mom was sixteen.

I believe this picture was taken on their wedding day.

Thank you, my heavenly Father, for godly parents.

Oh, what it would mean to me. Just to tell them I love you!

If you love someone, tell them today.

My Precious
Daddy, & Mommy

Gertie Mae Blanton
Black dress and Hat
"MY mother"

Aunt Myrtle
white dress

I believe this picture was taken
in the hollow where we lived

Lily Day
Basham—Blanton
She was Lakota Sioux Indian

Alonzo
"Lon"—Blanton
He was Scott Irish

My Grandparents
My Dad's—Mom & Dad

Top: left to right
Lonard, Billy, Leslie, Charlie
Center: left to right
Elaine, Doris, Martha

Precious Special Memories

- Not in the picture -
Wilodean, Edith, Alpha & Lealand

Ones deceased:
Lealand, Leslie, Wilodean, Edith,
Charlie, Doris & Elaine

Gearys

Busters Dad & Mom

Roscoe & Essie

Buster Family

Cecil—Busters Brother

Essie

Some of The Geary Family

Cecil & Linda

Vilma—Busters Sister

Marvin, Zelma, Candy, Wayne, Velma & Debbie

Buster

Me, Age 16

Donna & Billy

My Brother Billy and his wife, Donna.
I am so close to these two; they have been married
over 40 years and still are, so much love.
They believe in—Til Death do us part.
"My Buddies for life." They have three children;
Laurie, Jenny & Missy. God watch over and
keep them, for I have them dearly.
Billy and I have been very close since we were children.

Billy & Donna

young Billy

Missy, Jennifer, Laurie

Missy & Laurie
and their children

Stars

-N-

Hearts

Billy
when he
was in
Vietnam

MISTY MILES

Missy when she was in Real Estate

Billy, serving his country.
This Sister was very
Proud of him, "Still Am"

Faithful Soldier, Billy

I think he deserves
A purple Heart, so I'll
give him one.

Billy & Donna

Tony   Billy   Ricky

Memories

My Brother Leslie for right
And his son Donnie
Leslie has two other children
Ronnie and Dian

Sweet
Memories

left to right
Martha, Charlie, Deanna,
Leslie, Robert, Debbie, Elaine

About Alpha and James

Easy to
Love
This
Family

I wrote this for my sister Alpha and her husband James, 60th wedding anniversary. I put it in a gold frame. It now hangs on the wall in her room. I know she cherrishes it, after all; I'm the only sister she has left in this world and she clings to me, as I do her. And we both cling to our little brother, "Charming" Billy. He's not so little, but, he is our baby brother.

Alpha and James are beautiful people and has many many friends. Everyone who meets them, loves them. Their children are thoroughly devoted to them. In this day and time, thats rare.

God Bless Them Both!

left to right

David
Arlene
Kevin
James
Alpha (middle)

Love
you
All!

James & Alpha Helson
60th Wedding Anniversary

Happy Anniversary Sweetheart, my woman, my wife
Sixty years ago I put a ring on you finger,
Sixty years ago I met the love of my life.
God was molding and shaping this union forever,
Sixty years ago you became my wife.

Through trials and temptations, through the struggles
of this life, we've faced them together, me and my wife.
How sweet is the victory when the battles are won,
How precious our life when two souls become one.

Happy Anniversary, my husband
And always you'll be the man I adore.
Sixty years ago I put a ring on your finger
Sixty year ago I met the love of my life.
God was molding and shaping this union forever,
Sixty years ago you became my husband,
My dream come true, the man of my life.

How sweet it is to find someone to cherish
The way I do you for all of our lives.
Through happy times and sorrow you've been here beside me,
Through sickness and health, what more can I say.

The marriage vows, they are so precious, but how many people stick
by them today, we're so thankful that God ordained our marriage.
It's lasted this far, this love we both cherish,
And we know it will last for the rest of our days.

Written by: Martha Geary, your sister
April 28th, 2013

Precious Memories

Forever

(Left to right: Eric, Michael, John, Dillon)

There's that peace sign that's what we need more of press on Dillon Marlo & John

(Teresa, holding little Michael, & John sitting beside her)

True love, Whitney, Michael, Dillon

(Marlo)

(Right: Marlo, John, Wife)

(Dillon, Marlo)

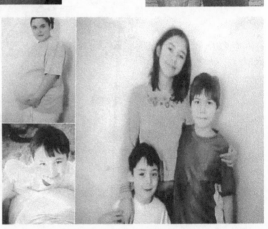

Precious Memories

John & Edith House

Johnny Franklin
Teresa Marlene
Deornis William
Larry Dewayne
Melissa Mae
Robert Jerome
Sharon Ann

Special People

Edith, my sister and her husband, John;
could not have children for seven years
after they were married; when they did start,
they had one for every year they missed.
They stayed together until death parted them.
They both are deceased.
May God Bless and keep their children.
John and Edith loved them so.
When they were here on this Earth
They made sure their children were taken care of.

Rest in peace,
My sister and brother.

Above are the names of all
their children

When Edith and John
got married they could
not have children
for a long while "I
was" their sorrigate
child. They lavished
a lot of love on me
I miss them so
very much.

My sister Doris and her husband Charles
and their children

left to right   top

Howard   row

Linda, his wife

Cindy

Marty   bottom

Chris   row

Lori, Chrises wife   left to

Howards baby   right

Doris—my sister

Charles—her husband

Precious
Memories

Charles was a minister
This was their church

Their children were:
Charles Christopher (Chris)
Howard
Marty
Cindy

Doris
&
Erica
her
grand
daugh-
ter

Edith and John

What A Special Little Guy He Was

Lealand

This is Lealand, my eldest brother
that drowned at the age of seventeen.
What a sweet little face.
I never really knew him—as I should;
But someday, by the Grace of God;
I will

I was only 3 years old
when he left this world
I have memories of him
Pulling my baby brother and
myself in a wagon.
He was a beautiful person,
I do remember that.

Memories, I do have some -
That of the three year old,
You'd be surprised how
Vivid they are.

Special
Memories

Treasured
Memories

Robert   Amy

Precious   Sweet
Memories   Memories

This is Lonards children
Memories
Pressed between the pages
of my mind

Lonard, 1978
Look at those eyes
Blue as the sky
Sleep peacefully my brother, I love
and miss you.

A million
good byes
could
never
erase
your
memory

I miss
you my
brother.

My brother
—Lonard

This is a birthday
card he gave me,
I cherish things
like this
I know it comes
from the heart

Lonard is deceased

Love is God
Shining

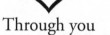

Through you

Happy birthday sis

Bobby

I know
Lonard
cared for
you.

Thank
you
Bobby
for caring
for my
brother

Bobby Pettyjohn—Lonards best friend
"Best Buddies Forever"

Friends

Best
Friends

Bobby & Carol

Memories

Uncle Bill, Aunt Fannie
And, Aunt Tommie

Love you
Daddy!

Wilodean is holding me

Dad and one of his horses

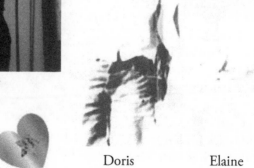

Buster and myself

Doris   Elaine

left to right—my best friends
Ruth, (Martha,) Susie,
me is my cousin

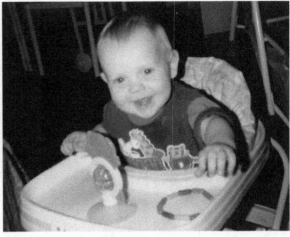

Tyler, David's son

Cody, David's son

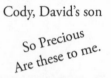

So Precious
Are these to me.

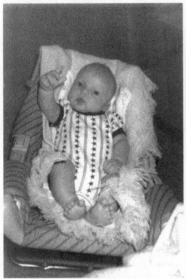

This is a special picture
to me—Brandon
My first born grandson, first
born grandchild period
We had a special thing between
us, when I said—"Love Forever"
He would stick his finger up,
so I would touch it with mine
How's that for someone so small?

Brandon
He is the one on the left
also. Our love forever
thing.

Shawn
Deanna's son

Miss you
Aunt Dessie

Lonard, Susie, Elaine, Martha,
Aunt Dessie in the wheelchair

Me.

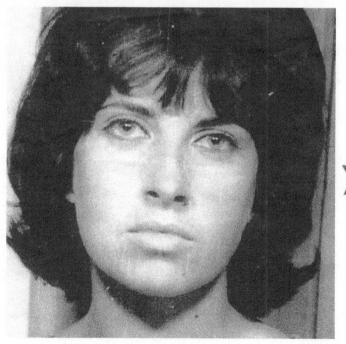

Someday we'll have another reunion
"In Heaven"

Me
with
the
baby—
Cody,
David
son

Donnie
with the
sunglasses
Leslie's
son

The Blanton Reunion

Precious
Memories

My brother Leslie in the hat—deceased
My son David standing—Lonard's son Robert
Beside him—Robert's wife sitting beside him

This is Charlie (Charles Curtis) Deceased
As you can see, he was a motorcycle
man. Oh, how I miss my family.
Charlie was alot like our Dad.
Fearless; never backed down from any man,
But, incased in that flesh, was a Heart of Pure Gold.
He would give you the shirt off from his back.
But you know what? That held true of
everyone of our Brothers and Sisters.
The Roots of our Raising Run Deep.

Cody
Charlie's
only son

His children are:
Stephanie
Tammy
Tiffanie
Cody

Stephanie

Stephanie and Husband Dickie

Charlie & Sue and Kids

Stephanie & Kids

Tammy and Husband Tony

Tiffanie and Cody

Cody Charlie's only son

Charlie's daughter, Tiffanie

Jeffrey & Alice

Heather, Alice, Jeffrey, Carol,
Bobby Charles

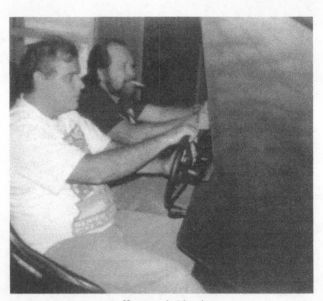

Jeffrey and Charlie

Jeffrey and Charlie were best friends—they grew
up together. They were friends til Charlie passed
away. Brothers best describes what they were.

Forgive and You Will Be Forgiven

I look around and, oh, what I see
There is so much sin in our world
She's reeling to and fro like a drunkard
The weight is so heavy upon her
Where will this all end?
Only God up in heaven knows
Blacks against whites, whites against blacks
Every race and creed is not exempt from
The hatred and sin within
All we can hear is the things they do to me
I cannot forgive
So the hatred, the revenge goes on and on
What about the Word of God, does it mean nothing
Anymore? God's Word says if you do not
Forgive someone else their trespasses
God will not forgive you yours
If you judge another, you'll be judged
Let us, let those words ring in our ears
And get down deep into our hearts
Every man, every woman, every human being
In this world is guilty of sin
For all have sinned and come short of the glory of God.
A man called Jesus wiped away our sins
By giving his life for you and me.
He paid our sin debt with his own blood
I ask you who are we to judge another man?
When Jesus was the one who bled and died
At Calvary to save us all from hell.

I don't know about you, but that means something to me
That means a man loved me enough
To die for me, he loved me enough that he
Paid my sin debt, a debt I owed that I
could not pay. Oh, I wasn't worthy of that
Hell should have been my home, but because he loved me,
He said, "No, I'll go for her."
And you know what? He didn't
just do that for me; forgiveness is there
for anyone, regardless of their sin
no matter how bad it may be.
I'm telling you, people—red, yellow, black, or white.
Jesus saw no color; he makes no distinction
Everyone has the same opportunity.
The sweetest words anyone could ever hear is
"I forgive."
I'm speaking to, blacks, whites, yellow or red man
We've all been mistreated by someone.
We've all been hurt some way.
I don't know about you, but I choose to forgive
When the judge of all the earth comes back
I want to hear him say to me, "Well done
"my good and faithful servant, a crown of
"Life you have won"
Those are the words I want to hear, not
"Depart from me, I never knew you"
I refuse to hang on to hatred that will destroy
Me and everyone around me.
Satan comes to kill, steal, and destroy

Lord, help us, what havoc he's wreaking
All because people give in to his lies
I beg of you, let it go, let the anger
Hatred and revenge go. Let it go.
Trust God to be your avenger
"Vengeance is mine," sayeth the Lord
"I will repay"
After all, it is he who died for all the world
All mankind, not us
Vengeance should be his, not ours
If you belong to God, if you have accepted
The gift his son gave; his life for yours
You are his. Whoever approaches you
Approaches your maker, and who can stand
Against him? If God be for you, who can be against you?
He who created the universe, the heavens
and the earth, is your friend.
He loves you; he loved you enough to send
His only Son to die for you. How much love
Do we need to see before we realize we're loved?
No matter what anyone, anywhere,
Any color has done to you, I beg of you
Forgive them, no matter how bad it may
have been, forgive them
Let vengeance be his. The favor of Almighty
God will rest upon you. May God speak
To your hearts as you read this
And grant you grace to forgive your enemies.

Wings of an Angel

If I had the wings of an angel
Above this old world, I would fly
I'd fly to the arms of my Savior
And never no more would I cry
If I had the wings of an angel
Free from this old body I'd be
My legs would not have to bare me
This old body's a prison to me
I'd soar over the mountains and valleys
Far from these pains in my soul
Up there, there would be no more sorrow
Straight to my Savior's arms I'd go
Lord, give me the wings that I long for
Don't leave me down here all alone
Give me the wings that I long for
Dear, Lord, you know that in this old world
Is not where I belong

Words of wisdom

Trying to impart words of wisdom knowledge
And understanding to a foolish man
Is like trying to feed someone who is
Starving to death for life giving food
Who will not open his mouth to receive it
So it is with any person
Who is trying to impart wisdom,
knowledge, and understanding
To a starving hungry soul
Who refuses his words of wisdom
If you are hired to do a job but you do not have
The tools you need to get it done,
so you may feed your family
This man walks up and says
"I have the tools you need. Here they are
"Won't you please take them?"
What are you going to say? Be on your way
"You are foolish to offer me the tools I need"
Or are you going to be wise and say
"Oh, thank you kind, sir, for caring enough
"About me, for helping me that I can get
"This job done that I was hired to do
"So I may receive my pay, my reward"
Words of wisdom received
Will most certainly bring their reward

Wings of a Snow White Dove

Life and times can get you down

These things are hard to bear

But when you're troubled in your heart

Just go to God in prayer

The windows of heaven will open

As he looks down from above

Then he'll send his love down to you

On the wings of a snow white dove

My Dream of Doris, My Sister

Doris, my sister, and I were standing on
a bank and buster was standing on the opposite side.
There was a stream of water
between us. The stream wasn't very wide,
but it was deep and calm. The bank on
Buster's side was slightly muddy, and on our
side was somewhat steeper than the side he was on.
The stream led to a drain hole that was very
strong once you got to it. The drain hole with the
powerful suction was big enough for a human to go through but
  barely.
Buster was waiting for Doris and I to jump across
to the side he was on.
I went first and made it across just fine, then
it was Doris's turn to jump across
I remember she had these white shoes on. They looked
like house shoes, very soft with just a flat sole on them.
For some reason, they really stuck out in my mind
They were so bright white, but I can remember thinking,
"These shoes has no sole to grip when she jumps and
"The bank was somewhat muddy but smooth"
I remember thinking, "They can't grip the bank
"And she may lose her footing"
We were encouraging her to jump
And somehow, I had a hold of her hands
When I said jump as hard as she can, she jumped
And when she did, she didn't jump hard enough
And sure enough, she lost her footing and went
backward. Her weight broke the hold I had on her
hands and she fell into the water, and it was deep.
It started carrying her to the drain. She was
helpless, caught in the drain. She got stuck
in it, and I was yelling for Buster to go down and get her

*The suction was so powerful that it sucked all her clothes off from
    her*
Her body was white as a sheet, but she was still alive
Buster jumped down and grabbed her. The suction was so strong
It was like he was birthing a baby from a momma
He grabbed her with both hands by her head and pulled her out
I remember her body looked like a newborn baby, naked and white
(Then it was the end of my dream)
As far as I can remember

My sister passed away not too long
After I had this dream
All I could think of concerning this dream was
A new birth for her

Heaven's Rose

Only sixteen, so lovely and fair
God picked a rose
He wanted her up there
Oh, how it hurt us to see her go
But God said, "It's time,
"I want my little rose"
How she bloomed so sweetly
Her beauty was beyond compare
This little rose called Becky
With heavenly blue eyes
And long brown hair
Her voice was like an angel
Now she's singing around the throne
In a place that God's sweet heaven
And we know that's where she belongs
"Tell Mom and Dad I love them"
I heard her sweet voice say
"Don't weep for me, I'm happy now
"Just bow your heads and pray
"That we'll all be together again in heaven
"Some sweet day, so don't be so sorrowful that I had
"To go away"

(This poem was written about a little sixteen-year-old
girl I knew who died in an automobile accident.)

CPSIA information can be obtained
at www.ICGtesting.com
Printed in the USA
LVHW020020310520
656910LV00005B/376